Lessons Learned...

Through No Words At All

parenting a child with
developmental differences

KIMBERLY KELSOE HAWKINS

"World Changers" — When I read these words in *Lessons Learned... Through No Words At All*, I screamed YES! I am also the parent of a daughter on the autism spectrum and use the term 'world changers' all the time. Unknowingly, children on the spectrum impact all those they encounter. Most people won't realize their softened hearts, increased patience, opened minds, etc. are the results of their interactions with a child on the autism spectrum. Think of it as a snowball – the more lessons we learn from the 'world changers' in our lives, the more we can pass on to others.

I had the privilege of working with Abigayle as her RBT (Registered Behavior Technician) during the 2020-21 school year. All of my previous school experiences were with preschoolers, so I was definitely out of my league accepting the role of RBT to a 15-year-old, non-verbal, almost-my-size child on the spectrum.

After a few weeks of Abigayle and I getting to know each other, we formed an amazing bond. Once our relationship was solid, she began to shine! I learned how to read her body language and interpret her sounds, and she learned the benefits of being compliant to the demands made on her.

Were there tough days? Absolutely! However, they were fewer and fewer as I learned how to apply many of the lessons Kimberly outlined in the book to my days with Abigayle.

Were there rewarding days? Absolutely! They became more and more frequent as Abigayle started to trust me and have fun during therapy.

As I read Kimberly's book, I not only thought of how these lessons are being applied in my life as the parent of a child on the spectrum, but I was thinking how the lessons can apply to EVERYONE! What an amazing world we would live in if everyone could live their lives according to the lessons Kimberly lays out for us.

I believe we are all unique, created in God's image and for His purpose. And the purpose for those with autism and other developmental challenges is to change the world.

Lauren Deman
Santa Rosa Beach, Florida

. . . .

I am honored to write this testimonial to Kimberly's new book: *Lessons Learned... Through No Words At All: Parenting a Child with Developmental Differences*. My testimonial is as brief as the length of time it took for her message to captivate my heart... and mind. The narrative is so matter-of-fact and the contents so worldly and human that hardly anyone will need convincing that this is a must-read... a page-turner, as it were. As I explained my grasp of the message to my own children, over and again, I told them the story reminds me of the essence of a telescope they recently bought me for Fathers' Day: that as the stars are seen best when it is darkest outside, so does Kimberly's story remind one that sometimes the shiniest of stars are only seen through the darkest skies. Through the many trials and tribulations she and her family have had to grapple with, she is able to recognize and document the many blessings rooted in those struggles... stars that would otherwise remain masked behind their many other blessings. In this book, Kimberly teaches us to grab hold of whatever we are fated with in life, and search for inherent blessings that would otherwise remain hidden. In this book, you will get to meet and fall in love with many of her family's stars—especially their dear Abigayle—against the backdrop of the real-life challenges of "Parenting a Child with Developmental Differences." I beseech you to read it: you will be appreciative that you did.

Ali B. Mansaray
Columbia, South Carolina

. . . .

The entire book was heartfelt and a wonderfully easy read. I found myself reading along, nodding my head in agreement with every word, and sobbing by the end. I love how Kimberly talks about the hard things but makes it a sweet and positive journey. Living this life, myself, I can picture the tantrums she writes about, having two of my four special needs kids who tantrum. This life is hard, but the journey is so worth all you learn from it and all you can give back to your children and others. This is a GREAT BOOK that I will recommend to every autism mama!!

Melissa Kramer, MBA, CPA
Founder/Executive Director
Growing Together Behavioral Center
Jacksonville, Florida

. . . .

Kimberly finds a reason for joy everywhere ... even in situations most of us would run from. Yet, as she reveals in this touching book, she wouldn't trade her life for anything. Kimberly has met the challenges of parenting a special needs child with uncommon courage and a creativity borne of necessity. That creativity has led to an inventiveness that helps others facing similar struggles in their own lives.

RJ
Editor

. . . .

Lessons Learned... Through No Words At All provides an honest and raw glimpse into the lives of those individuals who live alongside a person with developmental differences. Whether you've just found out you will have a child with developmental differences or you've met a new friend who does, this book provides hope and encouragement to all. You will laugh, cry, and reminisce with Kimberly as you ride alongside her on this journey into a new and different world – a world full of triumphs, patience, and tears. I recommend that everyone who is interested in learning more about what life is like for individuals with developmental differences give this book a read. You won't regret it!

Adrienne Seaborn
Board Certified Behavior Analyst
Behavior Associates & Bay Behavioral Group
Panama City Beach, Florida

. . . .

As a fellow author, I was inspired by the practical lessons that Kimberly captured so beautifully. As a sibling of a person with special needs, I can relate so well to her journey. What I liked most was her perspective on how her family's toughest challenges have turned out to be their greatest blessings. This is a book that everyone needs to read!

Samantha Lord
Author
Huntingtown, Maryland

. . . .

This book, *Lessons Learned... Through No Words At All*, drew me into a world of hope, tears, new expectations, and most of all, love. I decided to look it over on my phone before I got out of bed, thinking I would quickly glance through it. I couldn't put my phone down until I had read every single word. This book is about a sweet girl named Abigayle, but it is so much more than that. It is about this journey — not just Abigayle's, but that of her family, as well. It is also about Kimberly's incredible endurance. This book goes beyond what a parent faces with a child of autism. While it will be so helpful for those who are embarking on this journey or are in the midst of it, it is also helpful for the parent of a child with any disability. It is helpful for the parent going through the challenges of living with a teenager. It is helpful for the parent of a toddler. It is for any mom who feels discouraged, tired, worn down, and filled with so much love for her child. It is hope.

Lori Ellis
Co-Author of *Power Moments–Claim Your Identity*, by Jim & Lori Ellis
www.bookwithinabook.com

. . . .

I never understood the challenges faced by a parent of a child with developmental differences, including autism. Although the experiences she faces are frequent and intense, Kimberly shares her choice to find light and positivity through them rather than focusing only on the negative. This is a powerful story and good read for all.

Anita L. Parker
Lebanon, Tennessee

. . . .

Ten years ago, to the day, I met the most incredible family and have been forever grateful for all of the blessings I have received in return. I am Terese and I am humbled to have been so thoughtfully written about in this amazing book. I have learned about grace, patience, positivity, and strength through the love of Abigayle and her family. As Kimberly has said in this book, Abigayle is a blessing and my angel on earth. I have learned to be patient with myself, to not sweat the small stuff, to take time for myself to refuel, and to appreciate moments of laughter and calm. I encourage you to do whatever you need to do to appreciate yourself.

Terese Ghilarducci, MFT, PPS
Village High School Counselor
Pleasanton, California

. . . .

Perspective is the word that resonates with me after reading ***Lessons Learned... Through No Words At All***. Kimberly clearly articulates how, in the face of some of the most difficult challenges of parenting, she chooses to lead a meaningful life that is full of gratitude. She shares that it is not easy, but it is in <u>our own control</u> to make choices that align with our priorities, and to decide what things we need to let go of. She shares real-life tactical ideas on how to apply new ideas to my everyday life so I can live more meaningfully. Kimberly's capacity to help others almost seems boundless, and I'm grateful to have connected with her in my life.

Nancy Forsyth Hafstad
Reston, Virginia

Dedication

To my twin daughters, husband, and mom, all of whom sacrificed greatly to make this book become a reality. Without your love and support, this book would still be no more than a dream.

CONTENTS

Foreword xiii

Introduction xv

Chapter 1:   Our Story. 1

Chapter 2:   My Building Blocks 21

Chapter 3:   How "I" Do It All. 27

Chapter 4:   My Life Lessons 31

Chapter 5:   My Favorite Life Lesson: Don't Be So Hard on
             Yourself 35

Chapter 6:   Premier Life Lesson:
             Having the Right Perspective Is as Good as Gold . . . 45

Chapter 7:   "Here and Now" Matters Most. 73

Chapter 8:   External Influences Are on the Outside . . .
             Keep Them There. 95

Chapter 9:   Everyone Impacts Their Surroundings. 123

Chapter 10: Takeaways 129

Chapter 11: Who Has What It Takes? 133

Chapter 12: The Bright Side: The Tender Joys I Have
             Experienced Through the Love and Kindness
             of Others 139

Chapter 13: My Perspective 151

Chapter 14: When in Doubt, Just Have Patience and Give
             Love! 153

Chapter 15: Does It All Really Matter?. 155

Chapter 16: Don't Be Scared; Make it Count. 159

Chapter 17: Beyond the Bounds 161

Appendix I. 167

Appendix II. 169

FOREWORD

By Michelle Prince

I HAD THE PRIVILEGE of meeting Kimberly in January 2019 in Destin, Florida. She was an attendee at my "Book Bound" workshop, which is an event designed to help soon-to-be authors write, publish, and market a book. Kimberly made a lasting impression on me that weekend.

Most of the attendees came to "Book Bound" because they were excited to write a book and get their story "out of their head and onto paper." Kimberly was equally excited to be there, but I noticed that she was more concerned with helping the other attendees in the room find and craft their stories instead of working on her own. I witnessed her on many occasions having conversations with other people to help them get to the heart of their story. She was more than willing to give up the spotlight in sharing her book outline if it meant someone else could be heard. It was in that moment I knew Kimberly's heart—a heart that is the foundation of this book, her calling, and what makes Kimberly's journey as a mother of a child with developmental differences so special.

In *Lessons Learned… Through No Words At All*, Kimberly shares the joys, struggles, and practical lessons she's learned as a mother and provides insight into how to best navigate the challenges that come along with parenting. Many of her lessons came from parenting through hard times, and here Kimberly offers a blueprint for how to find the silver lining of goodness found in the struggle.

You will be encouraged, motivated, and inspired through Kimberly's journey. I encourage you to take these lessons and apply them to your own life. Parenting is such a gift, and the joy our children bring us is priceless. The hardships are equally rewarding and include valuable lessons that can change our lives if we're willing to embrace the process and enjoy the journey.

While the author's point-of-view comes from that of a parent, this book will benefit anyone looking to find a new perspective on the challenges we face in life and overcome and embrace all the beauty that lies ahead of us. I highly recommend you read this book and gift it to a friend!

INTRODUCTION

"**D**O YOU THINK I have a hard life, Mom?"

That question came from my daughter, Natalie. I knew she was referring to the challenges of being a twin sister to Abigayle, our non-verbal child with severe autism. "Yes," I responded, "your life may require more sacrifice and include more difficulty than the lives of a lot of other kids you know right now. The good news is that it gives you the opportunity to grow into a person with the skills and empathy necessary to thrive in this world." I further explained to her that everyone has difficulties in life and that this one is hers to bear. I reminded her there are blessings that accompany the pain, and we should focus on always being grateful for our life's blessings.

Natalie's question caused me to think of my own childhood. The challenges I faced toughened me and prepared me for the life I now have—as the parent of a non-verbal child with multiple health issues and developmental differences, including severe autism, cognitive delays, seizures, and a condition where she cannot cry emotional tears. It would be easy to dwell in negativity and only focus on the things I am missing out on, but thanks to my upbringing, I never stay in that mindset for long. It was my parents who taught me these valuable lessons growing up. Now that I'm an adult, it is my daughters who teach me how to live a full and productive life.

I refer to Abigayle as "my angel on earth." She entered this world with the strength and determination that even the toughest of warriors may not hold within themselves. Abigayle has many, many differences from the general population that are too long to list here, but you wouldn't know it by the level of love and happiness that she shares with the world. I am continually thankful and impressed with how she makes the most of each day. She truly is living her best life despite not having all the things that you and I so often take for granted—like the gift of speech. She does not let her challenges stop her. She takes on the world anew each day despite her limitations … as she does not seem to concern herself with them.

Abigayle has been creative teaching me her life lessons. God gave Abigayle the ability to speak just one word (so far): "mama." I consider this my personal gift from God to get me through the daily grind of life as a parent of a child diagnosed with severe autism. We don't know what she thinks "mama" actually means, because she says it all of the time indiscriminately. I have really treasured hearing her speak this one word since she was nine months old, but I sometimes wonder how much more I have to learn from her as she advances her communication skills—possibly through a communication device or pictures, or as her vocabulary itself might grow. She loves to say "mama" repeatedly and also loves to use "mama" as the only word for singing her tunes. She loves belting out in song very loudly, and often she will sing all throughout her day.

Abigayle goes through life with very limited communication skills. She has not been able to learn sign language properly or extensively due to her delayed cognition and fine motor skill limitations. She doesn't even have the luxury of knowing how to communicate by shaking her head "yes" or "no." Now, think about how many times you shake your head in a day as a form of communication. You likely don't even notice how many times you do so—to answer someone or reinforce your verbal answer—because it's *that* natural to you. Her vocabulary may be limited, but she hasn't let that slow down her ability to impact this world and teach invaluable life lessons that all can find beneficial.

"The best is yet to come."
William Shakespeare

Family.

Together.

Whether you are the parent of a child with developmental differences or not a parent at all, this book contains lessons for your life; they just happen to be things I have learned from parenting through some hard times. I hope ***Lessons Learned... Through No Words At All*** will provide practical encouragement for all.

"Do the best you can until you know better.
Then when you know better, do better."
Maya Angelou

CHAPTER 1

OUR STORY...

I HAD IT ALL!
I was newly married to George, owned a cute little house, and had a fabulous job in a field I wanted to be my life's career. I remember feeling guilty that everything in life was going so well and was so easy for me compared to other people I knew ... a kind of "winner's guilt," one might say. Then, for more than two years, my husband and I could not get pregnant.

During this time, I shared with a couple of friends on separate occasions that I could envision us having a child with developmental differences—as my husband and I are so loving, and because we especially LOVE kids. In hindsight, it seems so crazy that this, of all things, is what I was thinking while trying to get pregnant. I didn't think much of the statement, even forgetting I'd said it, until years later when my friend Shannon reminded me. Then I remembered saying it so clearly. Wow, the thought had surely been put into my mind from above!

The Miraculous Pregnancy ... TAKE TWO

In 2004, after two years of trying to get pregnant, my husband and I agreed that if "we" did not get pregnant by January 2005, we would start looking into adoption. While trying to conceive, and as a last effort, I underwent a very painful procedure to check everything out. The doctor told me that some people get pregnant after they "clean out the tubes."

Of course, I did not believe I would be "some people," so I didn't think much of her comment after so much disappointment in our pregnancy journey to date. Amazingly, we were "some people" in this case! We got pregnant in January—only two or so weeks after the procedure. It wasn't just any pregnancy though.

After trying so long to become pregnant, I finally saw the faint lines appear on the pregnancy test to confirm our dream came true. "We are PREGNANT!" I said to myself in complete and utter shock. I sat for a moment on the bathroom floor while tears filled my eyes. After taking a deep breath, I told myself again, "PREGNANT! We are PREGNANT!" I remember this moment so vividly even to this day.

Then, with extreme enthusiasm, I ran into the bedroom and woke George up in the early morning to share the incredible news and show him the positive test. He didn't believe it. Truly, he told me that the faint line did not mean that we were pregnant. He thought I was trying to see something that did not exist. To him, it was too good to be true. He went back to sleep—if he even had been awake during the conversation.

On my way to work, I stopped by an urgent care facility for a professional opinion. The nurse ran her own pregnancy test that confirmed I was pregnant, so I had her call George to share the news on speaker phone. (Looking back, it might have been better to wait for him to get at least one cup of coffee in him before sharing such life-changing news.) Even with the confirmation, I think he was still doubting it could be true after trying for so long and all of our disappointments.

After our first ultrasound, George was still cautious. He didn't want to get his hopes up. He knew things happened during pregnancies, so he could not relax until the doctor gave more assurances that we had reached a point where the odds were *for us* and not *against us*. During the first doctor visit, as we both sat there in the office waiting to hear his confirmation of our pregnancy together, I was quite anxious.

As the doctor shared all of the details about what to do from here and when to expect the new arrival, George told the doctor that he'd been out of town during the time I conceived. I'm sure the doctor had heard that joke before because he just kept talking. I gave George an evil eye for making such jokes with a stranger. George loves his dad jokes, but this was not the time or the place for jokes—in my anxious opinion.

The doctor confirmed we were having a baby and asked us to come back for a visit when we got a little further along (we were only around five weeks pregnant at the time). During the second visit, at eight weeks, we were getting another ultrasound when the lady performing it asked if we wanted to have twins. George started playing around and talking about how it would be great, and I told him not to jinx us. Then, I remembered and shared that we already had an ultrasound and only one baby showed up. I told them that having twins sounded fun, but it would be a lot of work. It turns out that I was right about that!

While we were having this discussion, I saw two circles on the ultrasound screen. I didn't know what I should see, so it seemed ordinary to me. Little did I know, we were about to be told that the two circles were two—not one, but TWO—babies! We were both in shock and very excited at the same time. It was very special to think that we were having twins, but I did not know what was ahead. My mom responded to the news by saying, "I knew it!" When our next appointment rolled around on April Fool's Day, I couldn't pass up the opportunity to call my sister to tell her we were having triplets, since each appointment a new baby appeared in our lives.

Outside of the typical problems associated with carrying twins, there were no warning signs that developmental differences were about to be introduced into our world. Due to a loss in our extended family in years past and our having twins, the doctor was very cautious and ordered multiple ultrasounds throughout the pregnancy—even a special, advanced one. Nothing odd ever showed up. I won't say that I was great at being pregnant or loved it, but it was a special time in my life that I will never forget.

25 or so weeks into our pregnancy, George and I had a huge scare. Doctors determined the girls were attempting to join this world way too early. Fortunately, the doctor prescribed some medication that helped stop the contractions. While it helped with the contractions, I ended up being admitted to the hospital with a bad reaction to the medicine. The doctors warned they would not be able to stop the contractions if they started up again, based upon my initial bad reaction. I ended up having pulmonary edema and stayed in the

hospital for a week. I was scared that I would have to stay at the hospital until birth, and I was also scared to leave.

The Neonatal Intensive Care Unit (NICU) doctors, and many specialists, were brought in to break the news of how we should prepare ourselves if the girls arrived early. The doctor said he felt the head of one of the girls trying to make its way out as he checked them. They told us horribly bleak stories—even today, I get sick thinking about them. It was heart-wrenching, but thankfully I didn't feel well enough to capture the full magnitude of the situation.

I was still a bright-eyed, first-time mother. I felt very sick, so I could not do much more than nod and listen to the devastating *possibilities*. I guess they have to prepare parents, but I'm not sure I needed to know everything that *could happen,* especially since it was out of our control. It only stressed me out further, which was not good for the babies or for my health. Even now, I think it was a bit too much and did not serve any value. Thankfully, the whole event was just a scare.

Upon release from the hospital—as an overachieving, hard worker—I was told I would have to stay on bed rest until giving birth. I thought, *WHAT??? How on earth am I going to do THAT? There is NO WAY!!! It's IMPOSSIBLE!*

Well, I was wrong, of course. As we all know, with God there is always a way!

> *"Fear not, for I am with you; be not dismayed, for I*
> *am your God; I will strengthen you, I will help you,*
> *I will uphold you with my righteous right hand."*
> Isiah 41:10 (ESV)

The mama bear inside of me kicked in, and I did an amazing job following the doctor's orders. I liked to move and was always busy, so when I heard I could only get up to take one shower a day and go to the bathroom ... I was worried. During that time, a peace came over me that allowed me to stay put. (Well, except for the multiple trips back and forth to the hospital when my contraction monitor gave us a new scare.) My goal was to reach 30 weeks, and then every week thereafter would be a blessing—at least that's what the doctor told me at the time.

"How did I do it?" you may wonder. Well, I decided I would live for my new bedrest schedule—one spent watching daytime dramas and talk shows. I took my schedule very seriously, as it was all I had to focus on since I couldn't work. It helped me survive—not the shows, but having a schedule to focus on every day. Before leaving for work in the morning, George would put several waters on a TV tray next to the couch, where I would stay until bedtime. That time likely prepared me for these pandemic days where many feel like they cannot escape Groundhog Day!

Every day, I would eat a cheese and sausage plate with seasoning from Rendezvous BBQ in Memphis, Tennessee, and tacos from the drive-thru at Taco Casa. I felt like I was going to work each day by *having* to maintain a strict schedule. However, as time went on and the house got dark and quiet, I did notice a change in my mood. Thankfully, after opening the blinds each day and having good communication with George, friends, and my doctor, I was able to push through the blues. This was my first experience with the blues, though I recognize it could also have been the hormones. Who knows? Regardless, it's something I never want to encounter again.

You may wonder how George managed during this crazy time in our lives. Well, let's just say he lost about 20 pounds in a few weeks and learned a lot about doing laundry. I started vomiting around the six-week mark multiple times a day. This continued all the way through until the birth, so it was interesting for George too. I remember once he placed a nice ribeye steak in front of me with a big, steaming hot potato. It was one of my favorite meals—but on this day, I looked at it and vomited all over the nice juicy steak before taking a single bite! Steak just wasn't something I could eat while pregnant.

Since I would get sick so often, I gained less than 40 pounds while pregnant. The doctor told me to eat anything I could keep down and to drink real milk-based ice cream shakes for the calories. That was definitely not what I expected to hear from a doctor, but I certainly enjoyed the shakes! The traditional ideas on keeping food down and nausea were not helpful for me—like eating salted crackers. Anything that was made by Little Debbie would stay down, although I never craved sweets before the pregnancy. I kept boxes of Little Debbie snacks beside my bed to eat before I got out of bed every morning. Somehow, eating Little Debbie snacks first thing in the morning really helped my nausea.

George and I made it to 30 weeks, so the doctor moved my goalpost to 32, and then to 34. We gave gratitude for each day we closed out with the girls still snug in my belly. Unfortunately for us all, there were some unknown challenges brewing just below the surface. We took it one day at a time, and many prayer warriors had us on their list. We felt blessed!

The Miraculous Birth

The twins were born by an emergency C-section at 32 ½ weeks. It was quite an eventful time for our family. The day before the birth, I went to the doctor for a normal checkup with my mother and was unexpectedly admitted to the hospital. This was the Thursday before Hurricane Katrina hit New Orleans. Right after being admitted, my doctor came in to tell me that she had to urgently leave town to pick up a child she was adopting from New Orleans. She assured me that I had a few days before giving birth and that she would be back for it.

Very early the next morning, the interim doctor let me know that he was "taking" the twins that day. He had concerns that my health would take a turn for the worse and that Abigayle was not getting the nutrition she needed. The doctor told me he would wait until 3:00 p.m. and no later for the C-section, since my husband was not in town. Just the day before, due to assurances from our usual doctor that we still had a few days before giving birth, my husband flew from Alabama to North Carolina to play golf at the famous Pinehurst No. 2.

Around 7:00 a.m., George got the call that he needed to urgently get home that day if he wished to make the birth of our twins. Another emergency on the floor delayed the procedure just long enough for my husband to run in from his flight at the very last minute. The early delivery was an unexpected blessing, because Natalie had the umbilical cord wrapped around her neck twice.

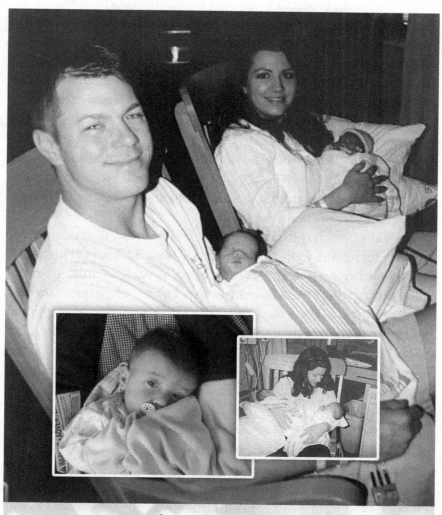

the beginning

The birth itself was not without its challenges. I could still feel things as they started the procedure. Since the epidural did not fully work, I was given another medicine that made me hallucinate. They did not tell me that I would hallucinate—at least not that I remembered. It all happened so fast. For a few moments, I thought I died while giving birth, since my worldly surroundings—like the walls—disappeared. After the birth, I was even convinced that George, who had a medical mask on, was someone else.

The doctors later told me that I was the funniest person they've ever encountered during a delivery. I still had some remnants of the medicine in me when they showed the children to me, so I thought Abigayle only had one eye in the center of her head. We never spoke of my hallucination and the one eye, but I remembered it vividly enough to believe it was my reality.

I couldn't see the girls for many hours due to the C-section. If my memory serves me well, I had to wait at least 12 hours. The family kept preparing me for how bad the girls looked (mainly Abigayle) compared to what we had seen in other babies. They never showed me any pictures of their faces, but I already "knew" that Abigayle had only one eye—or so I thought. Half a day after having my twins, I got to see the girls. To my relief, Abigayle had two beautiful eyes placed exactly where they were supposed to be. I thought the girls looked great, considering what I had been prepared to see.

Abigayle was the smaller one at 3.2 pounds, while Natalie weighed 4.7 pounds. Since the twins were premature, they struggled with a multitude of issues and required time in the NICU. They were not fully developed and suffered from jaundice, breathing issues, feeding difficulties, a severe life-threatening infection, weight loss, and more. Natalie was so fragile in her health that I was not able to hold her in my arms until a few days after birth.

I remember the first time they allowed me to hold her, which was when they were changing the padding underneath her. They only let me lift her directly up and put her directly back down. Tears of joy filled my eyes when I was able to hold her in my hands to lift her up while they changed her padding. The days that I could not hold her felt like forever to me, as a first-time mom. I wanted to feel her in my arms just once. Natalie met the milestones required for her discharge from NICU after six weeks. She has not suffered from any delays since then. Abigayle still had a significant battle ahead of her, including delays that persist to this day.

During the three-plus months she was in NICU, there were often concerns that Abigayle might not make it. I even had to comfort my dad as he cried at her bedside the week she was being released, because to him, she did not appear as if she would make it. I *never* doubted Abigayle would live—that is, until the first night we had her home, and she struggled to breathe. Within hours of her discharge, we had to take her right back to the NICU in the middle of the night.

I had to beg the birthing hospital's NICU—where the doctors knew her so well—to take her back, instead of taking her to the local children's hospital. She'd struggled with eating since birth, so we were sent home squirting milk from a bottle into her mouth to get it down. Sadly, she aspirated from the feeding the very first night I fed her on my own, and she ended up getting pneumonia. I felt like a failure. I couldn't get the squirting of the milk just right for her to get her nutrition. I was never good at it, but we were sent home anyway. I had to figure it out as a new mom on my own. I could no longer depend on the nurses to back me up.

When she returned to NICU a few hours later, her cleft palate was discovered. The doctors determined that the palate was causing her eating troubles. Abigayle weighed just six pounds when she was five months old. When the NICU doctors and nurses realized they had missed her cleft palate, they apologized profusely; it's something they typically find right away. Abigayle's long list of issues made her situation complex, and her medical team was always chasing one thing after another. She had many tests, which led to more and more tests, which resulted in fewer answers and more questions.

The Value of Advocacy

As Abigayle's chief advocate, it was critical for me to keep all her care providers and doctors on track. Sometimes, though, I was so focused on the day-to-day minutiae of Abigayle's care and taking care of Natalie as a newborn that I would lose sight of what was right in front of me. It was especially hard when—on top of everything else, including recovering from my C-section —Natalie had colic.

"Her smile and laughter can brighten our darkest day."

"Abigayle is here on earth to teach us all!"
Big Daddy

"Love her . . . and her chubby cheeks!"

Abigayle

UNIQUE GIFT FROM GOD

The first year of the twins' lives was acutely revealing, full of moments challenging to even the strongest of parents. One such moment occurred during a doctor's appointment when the nurse, having called Abigayle's name, tried to turn me away as I started toward her with Abigayle in my arms. She was looking for a seven-month-old baby, not a newborn, she said.

Wow! At times I did not realize how sick my daughter really was until, looking at pictures of her later, I saw how dire the situation glaring back at me truly was. I only saw what I *wanted* to see through my loving eyes. As a new mom, I only looked at her through a lens of perfection. While I know the reality of Abigayle's condition, I still can only look at her through the same lens to this very day.

Due to her cleft palate, we eventually had to make the difficult decision for her to have surgery and a gastronomy tube (G-tube) inserted to feed formula directly into her stomach. This was a true lifesaver for her. Even so, it was a hard decision for me to make regarding the surgery and what it meant. There were some additional risks in her ability to make it through being anesthetized with her unique physical features, which required special teams to support the surgery.

To this day, I don't exactly understand why it was so hard for me to make the decision to have her undergo the surgery for the G-tube. Somewhere inside me I thought of it as giving up. I thought I *should* be able to do it, and if I just tried harder, maybe I could do it and save her from the risky idea of surgery. I thought I was a failure for not being able to feed her like the nurses had. I really tried—but, looking back, I know it was not a long-term solution to squirt milk "into" a growing baby. Abigayle had the surgery, and, within a few weeks, she had chubby cheeks!

Months later, I offered to counsel other mothers going through the painful process of making the same decision. During one clinic visit, I was asked to counsel a new mother with twins who had to make the difficult decision for both of her babies, not just one. It was my pleasure to help another mother considering the surgery for her twins. It was another reminder to me that no matter how bad things may feel, there is always someone going through something more challenging.

After one year, Abigayle was able to have surgery on her cleft palate. The procedure was successful, and she could eat normally, for the most part. Since Abigayle could eat normally, she was able to have her G-tube removed. She still has some issues from time to time with eating due to her physical makeup, but it has mostly subsided. Abigayle will always suffer from gastrointestinal issues, but we are thankful to have treatments to help her get by.

Hidden Truths

Abigayle has some facial features that are a bit different. As she grew, her doctors noticed warning signs that indicated more was going on with her than they had initially thought. Even so, they continued to assure me that she was only suffering from obstacles caused by prematurity—from what they *knew*. However, not everyone was so sure. There was one doctor who continued running tests on Abigayle to find out what else was going on with her.

He didn't want to scare me without concrete answers, but her anomalies made him curious. Prior to her first discharge from NICU, he shared his speculative concerns with me. Her initial genetic test did not discover anything, which baffled him. Due to her numerous physical differences, he was sure there was something they were missing. As a first-time parent, and given her prematurity, I couldn't see what the doctors saw. Meanwhile, new medical issues continued to be introduced into our lives on a regular basis—for years.

Finally, after three years of medical tests and research, the doctors discovered that Abigayle had a chromosome abnormality that had originally been missed because of the unsophisticated testing tools used. The abnormality was causing many of her differences. Medical geneticists also diagnosed her with a rare syndrome that, we were told, could result in death due to heart defects and other serious anomalies. Just as we absorbed one challenge, another would come our way. (We still do not know what to expect long term from the chromosome abnormality. It was not followed or studied much at the time of her diagnosis.)

At nine months, on top of the many physical abnormalities and mental challenges, I *knew* in my heart that Abigayle had autism. It took years for her therapists to admit that she needed to be tested. Unfortunately, she wasn't diagnosed until she was three. The finality of the news that Abigayle would have a lifelong challenge was hard for me to accept and absorb. No longer could I *hope* that her struggles were caused by prematurity, or that she would "grow out of them." This was around the same time we received information from Abigayle's genetic testing. The doctors told us they believed the autism was caused by her genetic differences.

When I finally received Abigayle's lifelong autism diagnosis, I was driving down a road and started to cry. I use the word "cry," but it was so much more than tears pouring out of me. I would never be the same. The diagnosis was a life-changing moment that would define my family's future in a unique and unfamiliar way. I was young at heart, but I was forced to grow up beyond my imagined capacity in that very second to endure what was coming. In that moment, I learned how to feel through my emotions without breaking. I learned how to come out stronger on the other side. This helped me in later years during even tougher times. I fight to stay strong, because I know breaking would create tremendous suffering for my family.

You should know I don't typically cry, except for sentimental reasons (i.e., when I share about Abigayle overcoming hardships). I cried harder at that moment than any other moment in my life. Then, I accepted it, and I pulled myself together. I never cried again because of our new world of autism, but I almost always cry for others who find themselves in this world. I cry because I know it is HARD. I remember going to an orientation for families of autism at Abigayle's first school and hearing a father share his story of success onstage. Overwhelmed with emotions, I rushed to the bathroom and sat on the floor sobbing through most of the event.

I would not ask for autism for a child, but I thank God regularly for Abigayle being placed in our loving family. I tell people that if autism must exist, I am glad that we were chosen to provide the love and care for dear Abigayle. I could not be more blessed as I witness Abigayle's tremendous resilience in the face of adversity. While she has a long list of mental and physical differences, her severe autism diagnosis is the one that has impacted our family the most. It remains the center of our focus day in and day out.

True, Unconditional Love and Joy

Saying Abigayle has changed my life in so many ways is an understatement. In fact, she changes the lives of everyone she meets. It is so wonderful to hear the stories of bonding that others share with me after spending time with Abigayle. She really knows how to deeply touch a soul and change it for a lifetime, even during a brief meeting. There are definitely many struggles too, but my family is fortunate to have experiences that others will never have.

Abigayle has changed so many people's lives as they have come to know her and experience her joy, strength, and perseverance. She does not let anything or anyone stand in her way. She always finds a way to get what she wants! As she matures, things are evolving, and new experiences are creating additional depth in our love and respect for all she carries.

My bond with Abigayle, through all her medical and life struggles, became stronger than imaginable. Due to the many, many doctor appointments we had to go to each week, and after the months of NICU, I quit work and stayed home with the girls. It was a wonderful time, but the first year after their birth is still a bit foggy in my memory. I grew a lot as a person and mother that year, but it also made me understand what is and what is not important in life. This experience was just the beginning of my life lessons, though.

> **"Where there is no struggle, there is no strength."**
> Oprah Winfrey

I am so grateful for all that I have gained from motherhood, even with the struggles. When Abigayle looks into my eyes, I see her looking through them and into the greatest depth of my soul. When she embraces me, I feel as if we are truly one. Her childlike need for love gives so much to me. Her smile can brighten my darkest day! She's constantly teaching our family lessons. No one can truly experience a bad day with her love in their presence. It is all-consuming.

I'm so thankful that my family is loving in how we have responded to our uphill battles, and that I have a husband who is an amazing father for Abigayle. To this day, as she is a teenager, he changes her pull-on disposable diapers during her menstrual cycle or after her bowel movements. He does not draw any lines in the sand as to his responsibilities. He dives in for whatever is needed.

So many mothers find themselves alone fighting each day's challenges, which seem to multiply during the bad times. I am fortunate and know the value of what I have within my family. We all pitch in to the efforts and sacrifice, but what we gain is so much more than you can imagine looking in from the outside. I cannot tell you how many times people's first response is "sorry" when they hear of the long list of mental and physical differences we manage. I don't want to be pitied or consoled; I am thankful for what my experiences with Abigayle have brought into my life. There are rough and violent times, but the struggles never prevail over the gifts!

Sibling Sacrifices

Natalie, Abigayle's twin, does not know existence without severe autism in her environment. I cannot even imagine the effect it has had on her life, but I know the impact has been great. She has grown up in a household with daily tantrums, sleepless nights, and violent outbursts. For Natalie's entire life, she has put Abigayle's needs above her own—all day, every day. Abigayle also destroys a lot of things around the house, some of which are important to her sister. Natalie makes sacrifices daily and takes it all like a champion!

Natalie, who is what some would consider a typical teenager, understands that Abigayle's care and safety will always be our top priority. This means we're not able to make plans and do some of the things that other families do together. So many dinners and holidays have been impacted and interrupted by the struggles Abigayle faces from her routine being disrupted, being in a place that she cannot easily endure from a sensory perspective, her inability to communicate effectively, or because of the overstimulation of it all.

Safety First

Holidays like Christmas and Easter are quite different than with other families. Abigayle enjoys playing with and trying to eat the wrapping paper more than opening the gifts or caring about what is in the Easter basket. At Halloween, Abigayle does not understand the concept of trick-or-treat. Instead, she just tries to run under the offered candy bowl to explore every house. We also must be quite careful with what is being offered to Abigayle and what is in her surroundings. Abigayle has many, many allergies and is so fast at grabbing foods. It is all very confusing for her, not to mention the difficulty of trying to find costumes that work for Abigayle's sensory needs.

We have been to a few Christmas parties where Abigayle runs in circles and never sits down. Since other people's houses are not "Abigayle-proof," George and I follow her every step and stay uber-focused to make sure she does not touch anything, eat an allergy-related food, break anything, escape the house, or otherwise. It can be quite stressful keeping her safe on top of the fact that most parties do not allow Abigayle to follow her strict daily routine, which is always risking a tantrum. This is why most holidays are spent at home as a family, which can also be very rewarding.

Abigayle's day runs more smoothly when we adhere to an established routine. Change in her routine can be very difficult for her, and taking her on trips can be dangerous due to safety concerns. When we take Abigayle on trips, we must consider everything that Abigayle *may* come into contact with, how to manage her change in schedule with the least disruptions, how to keep her from being able to escape a room, and much more. Once, we had to stay in a hotel with her during a hurricane evacuation. We had to tell the hotel manager that we need to be called immediately if someone sees Abigayle wandering around by herself. It was hard to find ways to keep her safely in the room. It would only take a split second—going to the bathroom, or looking the other way—for trouble to find us. Others were worried about losing their house during Hurricane Michael's landfall, but I could only focus on Abigayle and her safety.

Since it is expensive and hard to find reliable childcare for Abigayle, it is also very hard to go on trips with Natalie the way other families do together. It is especially hard for George and I to find a way to take Natalie on a trip overnight to unwind, enjoy quiet time, and spend quality time together. This is especially difficult, as Natalie rarely gets a break from this lifestyle of constant alertness, which can cause chronic stress on the household. At times, Natalie endures more stress than many adults I know.

While some became familiar with lockdowns during the COVID-19 pandemic, Natalie lives in a house under lockdown all day long. To keep Abigayle safe, she always has to lock and unlock doors as she enters or exits her own bathroom and bedroom. If we do not lock doors, Abigayle will get into anything, and she can turn simple everyday items into something dangerous for her. I cannot imagine being young, having friends over, and then constantly having to remind them to lock the door every time they leave her room and bathroom, or explain why Abigayle is eating leaves or why they can't leave their drinks, food, or other small things left around that Abigayle could eat (anything really).

We all tease that no drink is safe around Abigayle because she takes great pride in swiping drinks all throughout her day. If there is a drink around that is not being protected, she will grab and drink it within seconds of walking in the room. She scouts the room for a drink and swipes them the second we look the other way. She grabs all drinks that are not hers, and it has nothing to do with thirst. She'll even grab drinks identical to hers. I've told people that she must keep a tally throughout the day, and she likely makes it a game. She is fast, sneaky, and successful.

Being a teenager, Natalie has so many other life events going on besides her day-to-day with Abigayle. She is experiencing this new world with its continuing COVID-19 concerns at such a pivotal time in her life, all while dealing with other teenage pressures. Her dad and I have been so blessed that she's such a kind and supportive teenager with her head on straight. She knows that we both have a lot on our plates with work and Abigayle, so she independently challenges herself to make great grades and grow in new ways. She continually plans for her future by making things happen to ensure her success.

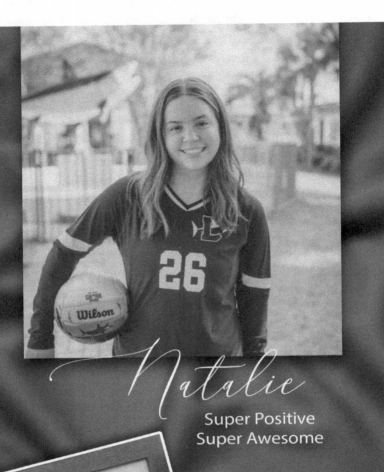

Natalie

Super Positive
Super Awesome

"Team First" Award
Varsity Volleyball

"Natalie is probably the sweetest person you will ever meet." - Coach

Rarely do I meet teachers or other people at her school without them complimenting the lady Natalie is becoming. Natalie has such an amazing heart because of her experiences. Her focus is less on herself than most people, and she is always considering the needs and perspectives of others. She must always anticipate Abigayle's needs, and that awareness carries over into other areas of her life.

Once, Natalie's grades were suffering because she was not getting enough rest. Every night, Abigayle was making such a racket that it was impossible for any of us to sleep. It was so disruptive that my husband and I lightly discussed having two houses—a separate one for Natalie's benefit and well-being. We worked through that time, and things improved through a lot of patience and communication, so we are thankful.

That's just a small sample of what Natalie has gone through. She is a true gem of a young woman. While Abigayle's life can be challenging at times, Natalie sacrifices a lot for the benefit of her sister and our family. Yet, neither of them focuses on what is *not*—instead, they live life the best way they can. I focus on the blessing of true, unconditional love; it feeds my soul and provides me strength to get through each challenging day ... one day at a time.

My blessings are many as I parent my precious twins. Abigayle and Natalie are both the sunshine in my day! Neither my husband nor I would exist as we are today without the girls just as they are and without all the experiences we have enjoyed and endured. We know our blessings, although sometimes reflection is needed to truly see them.

Life Has a Plan of Its Own

My husband and I were hoping to grow our family with a new pregnancy when the girls turned three, but life had other plans. We lost a pregnancy at 11 ½ weeks. The loss was gut-wrenching, serving as another life-changing moment for us. It was considered by the medical community to be an independent event unrelated to Abigayle's genetics (called a "fluke"), but it was scary to us when considering another pregnancy. Our having twins and Abigayle's multiple rare diagnoses were considered "flukes," as well. I remember asking my obstetrician how many "flukes" could happen in one family. She believed we were at our limit, but our family chose not to take any more chances.

The loss of the pregnancy, coupled with Abigayle's autism diagnosis at that time, gave us a window to consider what would be best for the girls moving forward. In the end, we decided it was better that we not grow our family, as we needed to devote every second of our available time and attention to Abigayle and Natalie. We understood that we needed to invest all our resources into getting the most out of life for our girls, bearing in mind the increased needs of developmental differences.

Our family is a work in progress, and we understand the value of savoring moments *during* the moment, rather than looking back as time marches forward. We moved forward without regret about not growing our family, as Natalie and Abigayle have and always will deserve all that we have to offer. As time has marched on, I know that we made the best choice for our family under the circumstances, and that life responded accordingly. I still have love for my third child whom I never met. One day, when the time is right, we will meet that child. Until then, I have peace.

> *"To live is the rarest thing in the world.*
> *Most people exist, that is all."*
> Oscar Wilde

CHAPTER 2

MY BUILDING BLOCKS

"Every day may not be good, but there's
something good in every day."
Alice Morse Earle

W E ALL HAVE stories about what it was that got us to where we are today and how that has impacted our lives. Time and time again, I have been asked to share my story in order to shine the light on the struggles, sacrifices, small and big wins, techniques for overcoming, and more aspects of my life to help others who are going through similar times. I never thought my story had much to teach anyone, nor did I think I could explain how I manage through the tough days. It all seems very natural to me. I have always felt gifted with a spirit of perseverance, patience, resilience, and the ability to not take things too personally. Don't get me wrong, I do struggle. I just don't let it all keep me down for long!

Diving into my story, I decided there are some nuggets to share that I hope will validate others and shed light on things in their lives that they never considered as part of their support unit for getting through and prospering in difficult times. Writing this material has given me a unique opportunity to discover how the challenging events of my past were gifts to prepare me for my future. Possibly, as I am almost 50 years into my journey of life, there is something in my story that can help others relate to their circumstances as they encounter their own speed bumps. Most importantly, I pray that sharing my journey can help others find a new perspective to help them on their own path and provide hope for a better future. If nothing else, we can all benefit from reading some amazing stories of acts of kindness and compassion from others in this book.

> ***There is so much more to who I am than the choices
> I made yesterday, but my choices are a great place to
> start to create a better life for myself tomorrow.***

My story began with many fun experiences as part of a very large, blended family in Missouri. I am the baby girl of many children, meaning I survived lots of teasing, chasing, wrestling, and games galore. My siblings toughened me up with all their more challenging behaviors, as well as their moments of protecting me against each other's teasing and taunting.

While I was born in Missouri, I lived in a few states before eventually calling the South my home. In the earliest days that I remember well, I lived on a farm, even playing with snakes, dressing our cats and pigs, and running up and down the dirt roads until dark. It's funny to think of these times now—I'm not exactly what you'd call a farm girl these days.

I moved around quite a bit when I was young (and later in life), which no doubt contributed to my ability to find my own strength, as I had to do with every move. The frequent moves were building blocks that reinforced my foundation. Each new town brought new schools, friends, churches, houses, and bullies.

The Bullies

Often being the new girl in school, I got the opportunity to recreate myself over and over and over again. No one knew my past—you know, the stories from pre-school that you never want repeated. Thank goodness social media did not exist to memorialize all those events!

Each new school brought much of the same "new girl" experiences. I had to hold my head high, as I was bullied and teased at each new school I attended. Thankfully, we had a large family, so I did not have to worry that all the friends were taken when I started school (which was not always at the beginning of the school year). I had to learn to be comfortable within myself, which is extremely valuable now that I am older, especially during COVID times.

Knowing that bullying could confront me at each new school, I worked hard to create ways to avoid getting attention. This was a futile effort, since I was typically the only new girl or one of very few in mostly small towns. People were interested in who I was and the places I had lived. Other people did not like that people were interested, which is when the teasing and bullying started. These episodes created opportunities for me to ignore the advances and not otherwise fan the flames of frustration of others.

I look back now and see how this has prepared me to manage Abigayle unemotionally during her tantrums. Even though Abigayle is now a teenager, she sometimes displays behaviors during tantrums that one might associate with a frustrated toddler: biting herself, throwing herself to the ground, hitting herself, banging her head, pulling at my clothes and biting holes in them, kicking, screaming, pulling my hair, scratching, and other physical displays of frustration. It would be easy for someone to react in an emotional or equally volatile way, but it does not help the situation.

In high school, I had girls throw balls of paper at me, threaten me, laugh at me, and say awful things. Again, this created an opportunity for me to not take their actions personally or react to them, as I went through this at every new school. I became very good at ignoring the behaviors and my surroundings. I had girls tell me they wanted to beat me up for the way I walked, talked, looked, and more. The bully typically felt more threatened than I did—because of my presence, they would lose something they needed desperately ... attention.

These moments provided me an opportunity to see the person from a place of understanding and sometimes pity. Being bullied is awful, but the experiences made me really see people for their struggle over my own. It also bolstered my confidence because I went through it enough times to know that I was not the cause of the desperate behaviors. I focused on myself and my reactions over the actions of others.

I understood that *I* was not less, as the bully tried to convince me, but the *bullies* felt less for themselves. They needed help. Sadly, bullies don't go away after high school. I have met a few in my professional career as well—though they use different tactics as adults. I'm sure I was devastated during the moments of darkness and mistreatment, but I have not carried the negative feelings into adulthood. That being said, I do have sparks of memories as I see these same individuals on social media—especially when they invite me to be their "friend." Not holding onto the negative feelings is a gift I've given to myself, one that is not about the individual with the bad behaviors.

These experiences only reinforce my confidence and strength. They create an opportunity for me to pray for the other person. I am using present tense, because, as I mentioned, I still run into a few limited individuals in my adult life. I have learned that people create ugliness around them when they are unable to experience validation, worthiness, and natural confidence because of who they are on the inside. We all have beauty within us to share with the world, whether we choose to see and share it or not.

> *"There's no denying the influence one life has on the world. In fact, sociologists tell us that even the shiest introvert will influence 10,000 people over the course of his or her lifetime. Our lives shape the people around us in profound ways. Whether we intend to or not, we affect others through our influence."*
> John Maxwell

Moving On

As an adult, I moved around a bit too. The place I have stayed the longest, so far, is Birmingham, Alabama. I love Birmingham! It's where I married George, found my first professional job, and bought my first house. Even though I left Birmingham in 2011, I still have friends and many fond memories from there. I really miss the amazing food and the crisp, cool weather in the fall, as well as football season. I grew into a woman and had my twins there—though, to be honest, I'm still a work in progress when it comes to the whole "growing into a woman" aspect. As I age, I realize that I am essentially still the same person, no matter the external growth.

There are many life experiences that have created new skill sets within me to manage my environment with Abigayle. Moving around and regularly being taken out of my comfort zone helped create a strength in me necessary for thriving in my current environment. I understand that bad things do happen to good people and that sometimes it is within our control, but sometimes it is not.

We have to make the most of our moments, experiences, and strengths. Every detail of our life, both the good and the bad, serves us by creating depths within our inner soul that are beyond our imagination. Life continues to mold me into a better person ready to take on whatever comes next ... when I experience struggle, I know it is a sign that I am about to grow in new ways. For that, I am thankful!

> **Strive to make today the best day EVER, and you will see that you are not missing out on the spectacular—you are creating it.**

Everyday struggles can sometimes wear you down, but I am extremely fortunate to understand what is important in life and what is just a distraction. Sometimes, a little struggle is needed to find gratefulness in tragedy. All we do affects others around us *and* our experiences. I don't suggest burying your feelings, but consider how you are experiencing them and if there are other perspectives that can make you feel differently.

Some people in similar circumstances as mine have shared that they feel like they are trapped—like being in jail. Others feel defeated. They question the WHY ... why me, why her/him, why now, why so hard, why not someone else, WHY? Instead, I choose to look at my circumstances and all the associated blessings. I focus my thoughts and energy looking at the good the circumstances offer me. I also look beyond the here and now. I look to God for my future beyond this life. My eternal faith in God gives me comfort that there is more to my experiences of the day. Because of Abigayle, I have made different life choices that have created a better life than I ever could've imagined for myself. I believe ... in God's perfect plan!

If I am tired or having a bad day, I try to either fight through it or take extra efforts to rest and get my mindfulness back on track. We all have more control over our lives, emotions, and thoughts than we realize. It's liberating and energizing to tap into the calm within by taking quiet time *without*—without all of the distractions of the day, without all of the noise—and to then escape into nothingness within ourselves to find our own strength and peace.

If I let the daily invaders to my happiness prevail and multiply, my situation will not have changed, but my experience of it will be depressing and defeating. If I let those little daily invaders win, my family will lose! If my family were to be infected by the negativity and destruction in the inner parts of my soul, then our collective negativity would spread to others. I understand it is critical to control my environment and influences so I can create a better world around me.

I remind myself that I own my days and my moments, despite how I choose to relinquish my ownership to my own detriment at times. I own my experiences … not because I control what comes at me each day but because of how I perceive what is coming at me and how I respond. I know I can choose to look for silver linings and respond with gratefulness for the opportunity to grow, or I can choose to let the challenge of the day defeat me. A momentary or past defeat does not have to define my future. I create a new path and move forward.

CHAPTER 3

HOW "I" DO IT ALL...

What Helps Me as I Cope My Way Through Life

L IFE WAS RELATIVELY easy during the beginning of my adulthood. When I didn't like something, I would just start a new chapter by moving to a new town, starting a new job or college program, etc. I would reset my environment and circumstances. It was fun to start over, essentially pressing reset. The strategy worked well for me when I was not responsible for a family.

With Abigayle and the rest of my family, I must take a lot of other considerations into mind before I can press the reset button on my circumstances. Now, I can reset my mind more than my circumstances, so that's what I do instead. Since so much comes at me in life (always what seems like at the same time), I have the "opportunity" to press reset and shift my thinking many times a day. It is an ongoing process as I continue to evolve to be the person I strive to be.

> *"You cannot always control what goes on outside.*
> *But you can always control what goes on inside."*
> Wayne Dyer

Today, there is so much hatred, resentment, and general ugliness all around us. Not only does this ugliness bombard me via news and social media, but I also have the everyday snags of life to manage. Besides that, I'm raising a child with increased demands and aggressions. In the years since the girls were born, I haven't really focused on the demands on me versus those of other parents; after all, this has been my only parenting experience. It is all I know. People tell me they can see the differences in our experiences, but I am of the belief that throughout our lifetimes, we are all stretched to our capacity in one way or another.

Recently, while talking to my friend Lisa, it hit me that my husband and I take care of all our own basic self-care needs and also Abigayle's—things like bathing, brushing teeth, getting dressed, brushing hair, bathroom needs, feeding/drinking preparation, and all of the other little things throughout the day. George and I basically share the responsibility of taking care of three people's needs collectively in a day, instead of just our own. I never really thought about or realized that before talking to Lisa. I logically knew it, but I never thought about all of the extra physical efforts in a day and the impact of those on our lives. It just hasn't been my focus when I think of my life or Abigayle. So, I laugh when doctors ask me if I am experiencing fatigue. "Well," I tell them, "it depends on your definition of fatigue and the source of it. No, I am not experiencing *unusual* fatigue for what my day offers me."

We are all our own unique individuals with our own unique problems and complications, needs, and coping skills. Life is not "one size fits all!" People have told me I have abilities to manage my circumstances in a way that they could not. When friends and family go through challenging medical, life-changing crises, they often tell me they know I understand. It is hard to say that anyone understands what another goes through in life, as we all have unique situations and skills to manage them. We also all have different support units and instinctive reactions that can make or break us in these critical moments.

While I did not choose the challenges I've encountered in my life, I can tell you that I would not choose anything else. All I have to do is talk to someone else to be thankful for my circumstances. All I have to do is look in the mirror and think back on how far I have come in life. It is a choice, though, as I could measure my existence and compare it to the perfect lives shown on social media. Instead, I think of the people in the hospitals and others struggling through so much more than I feel I could endure. I think of our history and advances that got me to where I stand at this very moment. For that, I am grateful!

My key to success is also managing my environment. Some days, it's so hard to keep up my positive spirit and energy when everyone

I encounter has low energy, bitterness, stresses, worries, and their own general concerns. That energy can invade my spirit, so I have to put on my armor to protect myself. Nothing good comes from being upset or worried, so there is no need to fall into a pit of negativity. Fortunately, I have many "go-to" people who can pick me back up. Yet, sometimes, I am the only "go-to" person who can exude positivity for others and myself.

> *"Do not let any unwholesome talk come out*
> *of your mouths, but only what is helpful for*
> *building others up according to their needs,*
> *that it may benefit those who listen."*
> Ephesians 4:29 (NIV)

My husband and I have learned so much from our experiences parenting our girls, and we are honored to have the opportunity to care for Abigayle's increased needs. We have learned to divide and conquer better than anyone I know. We both take responsibility by taking turns and focusing on where we can contribute the most to our family. For instance, George is an amazing cook. He loves picking out his groceries for cooking fresh every day. I am best at fixing Abigayle's hair ... over and over again throughout the day. Don't get me wrong, George makes valiant efforts in this area on days when I am not around or busy working. I even taught myself how to cut Abigayle's hair recently, since it is difficult for her when we go to a salon.

We have our delineation of some duties and share the responsibility for others, like riding Abigayle around in circles for hours on the golf cart. When I am hard at work or traveling for work, George does not hesitate to chip in more than his fair share to get Abigayle up and dressed for school, as well as transport her to and from school. He does this without complaint because we are a team, and he takes pride in being Abigayle's father.

> *"A generous person will prosper; whoever*
> *refreshes others will be refreshed."*
> Proverbs 11:25 (NIV)

In summary, help from loved ones and from generous, compassionate strangers is what helps me cope and do it "all." On the days where I have excess, I try to find ways to give to others generously and compassionately. It feeds my soul even more than being on the receiving end. We are not meant to handle the challenges in life alone, so look around for those trying to help you and who you can also give a helping hand. You may just save a life without even knowing it!

> *"For he will command his angels concerning*
> *you to guard you in all your ways."*
> Psalm 91:11 (NIV)

CHAPTER 4

MY LIFE LESSONS

All who have gone before us or are beside us now
have a story we can learn from. We should listen,
as they were presented to us for a reason. It may
not be for today, but it could save us tomorrow.

W HEN ABIGAYLE WAS born, my father said that she was
here to teach us all. He was so right, and he reminded me
of the value in her teachings often. Abigayle can change my mood
in an instant—just by looking at the joy on her precious face. She
endures so many obstacles that block her abilities in areas I take for
granted. What my dad did not know at the time was that Natalie
would teach me just as much through her response to growing up
amid the hardships.

Our girls have helped us evolve—as parents and individuals. We
must look beyond the here and now as we approach the more intense,
yet fleeting, tantrums and other stressful moments in our day. It
would be easy to just react and get caught up in the stress, but we
don't have the luxury of losing control of our emotions for immediate
release. This would only create more stress on the situation without
regard for what is important—Abigayle's safety, our safety, and the
avoidance of any unintended lasting effects on our relationship.

George and I need each other to create the best family
environment for our girls. We cannot afford to always act out in
anger when the moments get tough. We cannot take the frustrations
out on each other, as that would not do anything to help us cope
with our challenges. We are not perfect—we've snapped at each other
on the tiresome or more stressful of days, but we don't allow our
household to remain in a state of negativity, bitterness, and anger.
We get enough stress from the tantrums, so we don't need to add
more stress to each other's lives.

Our experiences with Abigayle alone have provided tremendous life lessons that anyone can benefit from—not just parents of a child with developmental differences. The lessons are numerous and stretch beyond just our immediate family. There are few days that those who encounter her do not mention her profound impact on them. Her joy and excitement about life are hard to ignore and infectious: when you hear her singing her own tune very loudly, or hear her laughing as she runs and jumps while flapping her arms around.

Abigayle's spirit is beautiful, and she shares it with the world. We have a saying around our house … "Everyone loves Abigayle." We say that, but that doesn't mean we don't encounter some limited individuals who choose to feel otherwise. We focus on the positive, loving encounters and pray for the limited individuals.

> *"I don't like that man. I must get to know him better."*
> Abraham Lincoln

In my lessons and other areas throughout this book, I share our family's stories and offer a small glimpse into how autism and other disabilities can impact families. However, my hope is that the stories I share touch a place deep inside of you and give you tools to make a greater impact in this world based upon your unique journey—not necessarily one of autism or parenting.

The lessons and materials I share in this book are for you, and my hope is that you can gain a lot from hearing different perspectives and approaches to many common struggles we all face in life—just like in the history books. You would be surprised how many of your common struggles are also being felt by others all around you. Even the strongest and most blessed among us have suffered through seemingly unescapable dark days.

I hope you get more out of this book than a nice read before bed. I pray that you get a glimpse into how we all have an impact on this world in a big way. I pray this book encourages you, no matter where you are in life, to contribute more love and grace into everyone you encounter every day from here on out. When I say *everyone* you encounter, that includes YOU! We will certainly have our dark days, but a smile can brighten even our best days!

> *"Learn from the mistakes of others. You cannot*
> *live long enough to make them all yourself."*
> Eleanor Roosevelt

When I was very young, I benefited from learning through watching the consequences of others' mistakes—most notably, the numerous and sometimes laughable mistakes of my older siblings. We are all a "work in progress" or we would not still be alive. Through my growth, I have discovered the value of learning from others to avoid experiencing the pain of always learning the hard way.

Let's Begin the Lessons

In the next few chapters, I will share some lessons I have learned that I hope will resonate with you. It is my desire to lift your spirits with this touching story about the love and perseverance of my life with my husband and our sweet twin daughters.

Now, let's discuss my favorite lessons I learned from Natalie and Pink Snail Abigayle (her pre-school nickname) through no words at all ... as she is non-verbal.

Insider Tip:

Balance is Key

As you're reading through the lessons in this book, keep in mind that changes and/or behaviors that tip the scales too far in one direction or area of your life can have undesirable effects ... like becoming a toxic fixation, creating insecurities, or stalling your progress altogether. I stress the importance of creating balance, as leaning too far one way can create new problems that require new life lessons. We are all navigating different places of our journey in every key area of our lives, so take this content in stride. Too much can literally be ... TOO MUCH!

CHAPTER 5

MY FAVORITE LIFE LESSON: DON'T BE SO HARD ON YOURSELF

THERE ARE MANY things in life I logically know that I don't always truly understand or remember as I go through the rigor in my days. I know that I am harder on myself than anyone else, but I don't always balance that with giving myself credit where it's due. Life isn't always easy or fair, so I must do the best I can with the tools I have. When I fail, I still learn.

> *"Any fool can know. The point is to understand."*
> Albert Einstein

In my personal and professional life, I find myself sharing this advice regularly. Many of us are hard on ourselves and try to live up to some image of who we *think* we need to be or what we *believe* is expected of us. I used to be a "wannabe" perfectionist, but letting those expectations go is now more important than ever.

As I have matured, I've come to understand that it's impossible to be judged as "perfect" by *anyone,* much less by *everyone*! This is both disappointing and life affirming. It's disappointing because we know we'll never achieve perfection. It's life affirming because we are freed from the need to strive for something that does not exist ... like looking for a unicorn!

I also know and understand that complete perfection is not achievable in the true sense of the word, as there are what are considered "flaws" in us all! Flaws create unique beauty within us. They are not to be hidden and rejected—they're to be celebrated for what makes us shine. There is so much freedom in letting go of the

ction and embracing our own unique attributes as being
l. I now see how comparing myself to others will do nothing
e than create turmoil for my soul and strife for my joy, so I resist
and think only of my own treasures. I am thankful!

Societal Strains

When I got out of college, I thought my house had to be perfectly
arranged with everything matching and beautiful. My house
resembles my image, so it was important to have it look nice—plus it
just made me feel good! I also used to put many hours a week into my
appearance. I laugh at this now because I no longer try to live up to
any image, except that of the parent of a child diagnosed with autism.
I hold this designation with honor.

While I love beautiful surroundings—a beautifully decorated
house, clean floors, groomed hair, and unstained clothes without
holes—that is just not my reality. In my world, I cannot have nice
decorations, as they can be dangerous for Abigayle. Abigayle throws
and spits food out anywhere and everywhere, so clean floors are not
on my priority list. Thankfully, our Labradors have always been more
than happy to pick up the slack and keep the floors free of food!

If I did keep a perfectly clean house, there wouldn't be any time
or energy left to parent and protect Abigayle, because her messes
are numerous. I cannot have plants inside because she likes to eat
leaves. I buy t-shirts at the local visitors' center for $10 and wear them
regularly, as most of my shirts are stained from caring for Abigayle.
She bites and pulls my shirts until they are ruined. I would go broke
if I invested heavily in my day-to-day clothes! Just this week, I told
my mom not to look down when she walked into my house, because
the floors were quite messy. There sure is a lot of love in my house,
though, of which I am very proud!

Abigayle can be quite messy, but she goes on like she doesn't have
a care in the world for much of the day (that is, when things are not
overwhelming her into a tantrum). She may have spit dripping down
her chin and food pieces all over her clothes, but we barely notice. She

primarily eats with her hands (or very messily with dinnerware) and loves to rub her food and hands all over her clothes.

At times, she will put food from her plate onto her belly before eating it. Sometimes she'll grab a big handful of mashed potatoes and squeeze it between her fingers before we can get to her. Abigayle has also been known to pull food out of her mouth to look at it and play with it before finally eating it. She even likes to put her empty bowls on her head like a hat.

Abigayle will also dig in her pull-on diaper from the outside of her clothes, which can allow leaks of her bowel movement or her cycle to become evident on her clothing. She has severe, chronic eczema and also digs for other sensory reasons. We have her wear jumpers to avoid the digging inside of her clothes, but she can still access some of the area by scratching outside of her clothing.

We change her clothes several times a day, but there seems to always be a drop of something somewhere on her. As I'm editing this paragraph just now, my husband is laughing and telling me that Abigayle is rubbing her hands all over his face and hair ... her hands, which smell like a hot dog from dinner. Now, he smells like hot dog! Others may not laugh, but I can tell you that she makes us better people simply for having experienced her with humor.

We say that her crazy, messy hair looks like a lion's mane. We brush and fix her hair repeatedly throughout the day, but it does not stay long. She loves to pull it, play with it, and mess it up as she squirms all around in her bed or otherwise. Many times, she has sat patiently for me as I have spent several minutes braiding her hair—only to immediately pull it out as I finish the very last touch.

Abigayle often rests on the floor in stores or when she is giving blood at the hospital. She does not care how her actions, hair, or anything else looks to others. She just lives her life as she decides and according to her own rules ... or lack thereof. Her smile tells me that she is not concerned with how others feel about her choices, many of which may not be considered "acceptable" in society.

Just **chillin** as a
Beach Bum!

Picture Credit:
Courtne Key

Abigayle LOVES when we tell her she looks fancy and pretty, which we do often. She enjoys this despite how she looks, and she does not have the pleasure of arguing with the comment. She cannot share that she hasn't washed her hair today, and it just looks awful, when we comment on how beautiful it is ... a compliment she hears often. She just smiles and smiles; as you can tell, her confidence abounds. She epitomizes true love!

Oh, and as for my hair: Abigayle pulls it with both hands while biting it. She twists it and plays with it. Recently I had my hair fixed nicely, and immediately afterwards Abigayle went into a tantrum. The result was that my beautifully styled hair ended up sticking up several inches in all directions, as if I had just touched electricity. Even this week, I could sense the odor of Abigayle's bowel movement following me around. I changed my clothes and double washed my hands before a quick sniff of my hair told me where the smell was originating from—yes, it was from my hair!

As I'm editing this book, I saw a past post on social media sharing a story about Abigayle throwing a sliver of American cheese. We looked everywhere for it but never found it. Well, you've probably guessed by now ... I later found it smushed in my hair! So, when I am home, my hair typically stays in a baseball cap or a bun to avoid having it within her easy reach. Earrings and jewelry are never worn unless I am not with Abigayle. This is my reality, but I am not a victim. It just ... *is*.

When I memorialize my day-to-day with Abigayle in social media forums, I share the good and some mitigated harsh realities. When I share things, I don't get too detailed about all that is going on in our lives. I just feel it is too much, but I balance that with a need for awareness that can cause people to take action and help those in similar situations without the resources I can access.

I sometimes think people don't want to see images that are not picture-perfect. I share many photos of Abigayle smiling, laughing, and playing, but I avoid the tantrums as a showcase. Tantrums are a huge part of our lives, but they are not what is featured. There is a reason for that, but it must be said that the pictures displayed in any household are not always the raw reality. I have even kept my disclosures of the day-to-day struggles a bit light here in the book, as this is not a book meant to educate on the harsh realities of severe autism and management of other disabilities. I am so much more fortunate than most, but there is a definite need for more to support our families and communities for children diagnosed with autism.

Reality is different, but as they say … how do you know good without the struggle? I could share the struggle more, that's true. I choose to look for and share the good in my life, so that it can multiply. As I said, everything requires balance. Awareness can be positive, but we all know that too much detail can drive people beyond their limits or can create more negativity in the world.

Because of my experiences, I give myself a break from living up to what I see on social media or in friends' houses where everything appears beautifully arranged. If you love me, you will love our house as it is and not as I stage it to be. I can say there is a lot of love in my household, for which I feel blessed. There are just not enough hours in a day to keep a perfectly clean house, groom myself lavishly, and parent my children according to my highest standards. If I worried about not meeting certain superficial criteria, I would stay depressed. Instead, I give myself a break and just do my best.

Now Put the Lesson to Work in Your Own Life ...

My Favorite Lesson Learned:
Don't be so hard on yourself

I've learned not to be too hard on myself. While that's important, it is also important to create balance in your life and not be too soft either. Take some time to consider how you need to create change in certain areas for your own benefit and that of the greater good.

We all have our hardships in life and choices to make regarding what we showcase to the world or when we ask for help. There are the normal life struggles and those that rock our world. Life is HARD, even for the strongest among us. Find the time to give yourself a break today and every day! Also, if you don't already have one, find a person who can be your trusted confidant. A non-judgmental and deep listening ear can change your life.

We are all constantly evolving as we navigate life. There is a constant need for us to step back in this fast-paced world and recognize our growth to see what we're capable of doing. Too often, I see people not giving themselves credit for who they are and what they have achieved or how they have grown. Without credit, there is no confidence for what they can do and where they can go in life.

What are some areas in your life where you need to give yourself a break, allow forgiveness, or give yourself some credit?

- Life is so much harder than we give ourselves credit for, and no one is perfect.
  CAVEAT: I tell my husband that I am perfect! ☺
- We all make mistakes and have regrets as we walk our journey. These mistakes don't define us—they create our depth of spirit. With this growth, we can give more to the world and be an example of overcoming to others. This is so important, as there will always be people behind us falling into the same mistakes or destructive patterns who could use an inspiring story to pull themselves back up and out for a better way of life.

- Do you have someone with whom you can share your struggles and who can support your journey toward reaching a better place? If not, seek out such a person. Pray to be matched with just the right soul to support your path.

What are some areas of your life where you need to relax a bit?

- When was the last time you took a relaxing vacation where you had "me time" or took deliberate efforts to be alone with your thoughts, relax, and recharge? What's holding you back? If it's a real obstacle, then find a way to plan around it and take inspired action to achieve your goals.
- What are the most stressful areas in your life? If they are beyond your control, then how can you create a different way of looking at them so that they can become your least stressful problems? Sometimes, it's as easy as just accepting the situation for what it is and working around it, rather than fighting it.
- Sometimes, good is good enough! I have a friend who is a perfectionist. It took her weeks to get a few sentences to me for a testimonial. The tweaking of her few sentences probably made it worse, and not better, over time. Sometimes we just have to go with good and not great on things!

Do you like what you see in the mirror—both on the inside and the outside?

- First and foremost, kindness can go a long way, especially when you give it as a gift to yourself and watch it spread to others around you. Whether you start big or small, just start showing and giving yourself little acts of kindness every day.
  - Buy yourself flowers, take a quick nap, or go get a massage.
  - Show yourself kindness by booking a vacation or buying yourself a new car.
  - Buy the fancy shoes or purse you've been wanting, but which you didn't buy because you thought you weren't worthy

of something so expensive and frivolous. Sometimes, we have to pamper ourselves to lift our spirits and multiply our feelings of goodness within. So, that pair of shoes is more than just for your feet—it feeds your confidence and so much more within you.

- o Take just ten minutes a day of alone time that you weren't previously allowing yourself.

- o Go after what you want, and enjoy the ride! You deserve anything in your dreams, so take that cooking class, move to the beach, invest in your passion, or do whatever else you can to bring more joy and love into your days.

- If you don't like what you see or what's on the inside, what changes can be made to get you to where you are happy and reveling in your own presence?

  - o I have to make myself feel beautiful and relish that beauty even on the days when I don't see the beauty reflected in the mirror. Everything about us is beautiful, as it is all a miracle that we exist ... everything about us is a miracle!

  - o If you're unhappy on the inside, consider creating opportunities to help support and give to others. By helping others, your own spirit will be lifted, and the world around you will improve. When thinking about whom you can contribute your time and resources to, the act of identifying the needs of others can have a positive effect on how you view your own situation.

  - o Another option for you may be more "me time" to reflect and create change.

  - o Counselors can give ideas and provide the support needed to adjust our thinking. Consider making an appointment.

- If you are unhappy on the outside, what are you doing currently to create changes in what you see?

  - o Are you sure that it is not really what's on the inside that is making you feel badly about what you see on the outside? Sometimes, when we create change on the inside, our view of the outside also changes.

- What can you start to do today to create changes in the areas identified as impactful for a better future? What have you been putting off that can positively impact this area?
- Question your perspective … are you being realistic and fair in your evaluation and expectations of yourself? Are you discounting what you have for what is not … like youth over wisdom?
- What are three things that you love about yourself? If it is hard to think of three things, consider what others compliment you on, or ask a friend what they love about you.
  - Start showing love and appreciation for yourself today. Continue this every day by writing three things down each night before you go to bed. As you do this, try to only repeat one item each day in the week. Explore yourself deeply and learn to celebrate what is so great about YOU!

Reminder: Don't be so hard on yourself

CHAPTER 6

PREMIER LIFE LESSON: HAVING THE RIGHT PERSPECTIVE IS AS GOOD AS GOLD

I WAS RAISED BY two of the most generous, positive, and kind people I've ever known. They showed me how to change my perspective so I could view things in a positive light and not through the darkness of negativity. My dad taught me how to maximize my present by dreaming big and often. My mom made sure none of the difficulties I faced were wasted. She set a high bar for me on how I responded to life's challenges. This really helped build a foundation in me that set me up for success in later years.

When someone was unkind to me, Mom always encouraged me to think about their circumstances and how bad things must be for them to behave the way they did. She helped me see others from a place of compassion. This approach helped me choose to live a happy existence rather than absorbing toxicity with every negative interaction. As an adult, I now understand that people go through different levels of pain for the same problems. They manage based upon their own ability to cope and skills they have learned for responding to life's big and little obstacles. I have learned in life that I cannot be the yardstick by which I measure others, nor can I let others be my yardstick.

"Being kind is more important than being right."
Andy Rooney

My perspective was really tested during the early days of Abigayle's challenges, especially when I was down or tired. At one point, the doctors did not know if Abigayle would ever walk, and there was concern over her hearing and vision, among other things. We are blessed that, among her many challenges, she was given the ability to walk steadily, see, and hear. I celebrate those things.

The world can be a very dark place, full of countless opportunities to be a victim or stay down in the dumps. Our environment offers plenty of chances for us to reinforce and validate the good in life, or the bad. During the tough times, I remind myself of walking the halls of the local children's hospital and seeing so many kids who were worse off than my own child. It's a reminder to me that good health and life itself are gifts, so I must not take them for granted by worrying about *what is not*. If I do that, I'll lose the ability to celebrate *what is*. So, instead of looking for what is wrong or missing, I look for the blessings!

Now, Put the Lesson to Work in Your Own Life ...

Premier Lesson Learned:
Having the right perspective is as good as gold

***We are here on earth to grow ... the alternative is
stagnation, which will slowly suffocate the life out of us.***

One of life's greatest gifts is to really know ourselves at the core of our soul. Learning more about who we are, and the depths of what we can do, can be life changing. We are so much more than we give ourselves credit for being.

How can you get to know yourself better?

- Make a promise to yourself to take 5 to 10 minutes a day to go within and get to know more of who you are and what is in your dreams. Write your dreams down, then start working towards them for a better tomorrow. Take a step forward, any step ... big or small. Just begin by taking inspired action. Remain flexible for what is presented before you as you progress towards your dream(s).
- One of the greatest perspectives we can gain in life comes from deep within us, where we dream big.

> *"You can discover more about a person in an
> hour of play than in a year of conversation."*
> Plato

Do you take the time to play anymore? How much, and what kind of play?

- If so, what are you learning about yourself in your hour of play?
- If not ...
  - What does that say about your effectiveness in life and your priorities? Life is so much more than work and

47

productivity. More advanced productivity will come with more time spent on play than without it.

- o   What did you do for play as a child that you enjoyed? How can you incorporate that activity back into your life?
- o   Playtime creates so much within us. It can also sometimes be a great form of much-needed exercise—either for our brain or our physical bodies.

How is your perspective impacting the way you view and experience your life today?

What are you thinking about most of the time? Are you stressing about life or celebrating it for its natural luster and its ways of always making things work out for good—both big and small?

- •   We cannot live happily while spending our moments focused on all the hardships and worry about what may be in the future. Life is full of miracles and surprises in the present ... right in front of us, right now.
- •   Our passions and talents exist for a reason. Are you using them to create a better world and future? Alternatively, are you letting them waste away?
- •   Each moment is a gift ... a present, as the saying goes.
- •   Are you dreaming for more or stressing for less? How is that working (or not working) out for you? What outcomes are you gaining in exchange for how you are spending your thoughts and time? Are you counting your blessings, or are you focused on what is missing in your life?

To live life to the fullest, commit to looking at the bright side of your circumstances for at least 80 percent of the time. Try this for a week and then watch it multiply!

Reminder: Having the right perspective is as good as gold

Life Lesson: The Little Things Matter

Many people ask if Abigayle will ever talk. They ask what is "the most" we can expect from her over her lifetime. We honestly don't know. All we know is that she is a very special and unique gift from God. At 18 months, her pediatrician said that she was going to stop guessing what Abigayle's limits were because Abigayle had already surpassed everything the medical experts thought she would ever do in life.

you can do it

"Every time we start thinking you won't
do something, you do it!
I love it! You are so "Hawkins."
(Letter from Mom to Abigayle)

49

Abigayle had so many scary encounters that could have ended badly, but she has a level of perseverance I've rarely seen in others. Babies next to Abigayle died from some of the same struggles through which Abigayle persevered. She is stubborn, which really helps her outcomes.

Abigayle sometimes makes a few leaps in her physical body, abilities, or cognitive levels, but other times she will make small changes over long periods of time. More recently, I have been amazed at how dramatically Abigayle has grown physically. When she was an infant, we were told that she would be unusually short. She also spent many years in a category doctors label "failure to thrive." Being the tough cookie she is, she is thriving. Today she is almost as tall as I am at 5'5"!

> **"Do not despise these small beginnings, for the**
> **Lord rejoices to see the work begin…"**
> Zechariah 4:10 (NLT)

Even at 16 years old, Abigayle is considered to have the cognitive level of a 12- to 18-month-old child in many of her interests and abilities. For instance, for entertainment, she watches animated movies and plays with toys that are meant for toddlers. We are thankful to have recently seen a huge jump in her abilities through her advances as a result of therapy. Only God knows Abigayle's potential, and I enjoy seeing her grow right before my eyes each and every day, inch by inch.

A tantrum can erupt any moment without provocation or any warning, so when we have our good moments and days, we celebrate them. Looking at Abigayle's smile and hearing her laughter—those are the things that get my family through the bad times. Don't get me wrong, there have been quite a few days when George and I count down the minutes until we can find some peace from the violent behaviors, tantrums, and other physical challenges (fingers crossed she goes to bed and sleeps through the night). What keeps us going strong is that we always try to look for those special in-between moments in life to relish, and I encourage you to do the same because they are all around us.

The Time to Treasure the Little Things in Life Is Today

Some days, when things are not so great, or when I'm really tired from life, I purposefully look up (ideally outside) and find miracles in my surroundings. For instance, if I'm driving, I look up at the sky or look at trees to find their unique beauty, and I am thankful. Other days, I take a few minutes to soak up the sunshine to remind myself there are miracles all around me—all I have to do is look for them. We cannot let moments go by wasted even during the toughest of times and darkest of days; we may find that we are out of time before we know it.

It is not only the little moments in life that can get away from us and be taken for granted. Abigayle does not have a lot of the luxuries in life that others have (like being able to decide what she will eat for dinner, what she will wear today, or even what she will do from moment to moment). Since she cannot communicate in words, much of her day is decided for her.

Abigayle won't complain or express her unhappiness about what kind of car we buy for her, because she won't be driving one. She does not whine for us to take her on a trip or buy her the newest and most popular cell phone or video game. Instead, she only worries about her priority needs and enjoys life as it unfolds … without any direction by her as to where she is going. She truly lives happily in the moment more than anyone else I have ever known. As the legendary Alabama football coach Nick Saban always says, "Be where your feet are."

> **The value we place on the little things will**
> **naturally expand through the grind of life chipping**
> **away at what is perceived to be important,**
> **yet later discovered to be otherwise.**

George and I have learned to be grateful for all that our unique journey adds to our lives. It took me many years to understand that I will not be better "when" this or that happens. Instead, it is important that I focus on appreciating *what is* today. I will only be better when I DECIDE to make things better with what I have and where I am.

51

We need to treasure the little moments for what they bring when they are here, not years later when they are gone. College is coming much too quickly for Natalie, so I am even more cognizant of the fleeting time as her graduation is approaching. Each day's ending makes it one day closer to her leaving home.

Abigayle's challenges are lifelong, so there is not a "when" where things will become easier. Her "when" may never come, in some cases. I cannot wait for when Abigayle can talk or is potty-trained, for instance. We just don't know, so we cannot live for what is not. We must appreciate all the little wonders of her experiences as they are now. This is why we must look within to find other solutions to live our best days and take advantage of the gifts all around us. To make the most of life, I focus on the good all around me, and I manage the rest.

Lifting Life Through Our Words and Actions

While Abigayle cannot talk, she can hear what people say. She also seems to have a special and supernatural sensory gift to know the true heart of a person when she is in their presence. It is as if she is not letting the words she hears get in the way of what she feels about a person. I wonder how much I miss by not cluing into the little details of my interactions with others.

It's hard for people to think of someone who cannot talk as someone who can *also* hear and understand most of what they say to her. Abigayle is so funny—when you talk about her in front of her, she loves to listen to every word. You can look at her face and see her listening to every single syllable. She will even stop singing to make sure she doesn't miss a thing.

On one of the girls' birthdays, I received a message from two family members singing "Happy Birthday" to Natalie alone. It did not occur to them to include Abigayle in their birthday message, even though they are twins. People often ask how to sign "you are welcome" after Abigayle signs "thank you." I explain that she can hear, even though she cannot speak. Over the years, we have also found that many sitters could not manage the quiet very well. They don't know what to do with themselves in her presence, since she cannot interact in the same way that you and I do. They forget, or never consider, that Abigayle has a need for interaction. It really shows someone's heart when they engage Abigayle.

Abigayle has little ways of letting me know when she needs her own private and quiet time. Otherwise, she loves when people engage with her. Like everyone else, she loves the little things in life ... like people telling her she did a good job and is pretty. She loves to hear herself sing too! Abigayle has a big presence and owns her space, so she is not one to pity. She gives so much love through no words at all!

Now Put the Lesson to Work in Your Own Life …

Lesson Learned:
The little things matter

I have learned that little things matter. Take a few minutes to discover more of the little things all around you.

I savor the sweetness of life. Abigayle's smile and Natalie's hugs are my go-tos for resetting myself during life's struggles. When you look for and relish the little moments and gifts, they can really stack up to a perfect day and life.

What are some of the big or little areas of your life that you can celebrate today?

- I celebrate my very breath. Do you?
- What are you doing with the life, including talents and passions, you have been given?
- On my down days, I celebrate that I showed up and made the most of my day with what was available to me. Can you say the same?
- It is always a time to celebrate!!! For instance, at the end of every summer when Abigayle would go back to school, George and I celebrated that we made it through another summer with Abigayle out of her routine and with the increased demands on us. Fortunately, now that she is attending South Walton Academy, she will be in therapy and school most of the year and, most importantly, on the same schedule almost all year long. Other schools had a different schedule during the summer season, which was confusing and challenging for Abigayle. As you may remember, her routine schedule is important to her.
- We should always celebrate and show love for the wonderful people in our lives. We may not have tomorrow with them in the same way as we do today.

- It's so important to celebrate every win in life as the moment occurs, as we never know when the next win will happen.

What little miracles are around you at this very moment? Expect miracles and you will experience them!

- Let's shift our thinking to the little gifts in life all around. If we do that, they will multiply! Look around and experience what you see at this very moment, because all our moments are meaningful.
- *We* own our happiness—or lack thereof—and we must live for the moments and enjoy all the little miracles in our day ... whether the sun is shining or rain is pouring onto the earth, these are miracles when you think about what they provide for us and everything that is required to make them come to pass. Then, just think about everything that had to happen for you to exist in order to observe that exact moment in that exact spot and time.
- We all need to take what we get and celebrate it, moment by moment and inch by inch. The future is not promised to anyone.

Reminder: The little things matter

Life Lesson: Life is grand, if you don't know any better

There have been so many times that Natalie and I have discussed how we wish we had Abigayle's ability to live life to the fullest—in between tantrums—without any concern for what else is going on in the world. Abigayle has many physical issues and health concerns, yet she lives more happily than most people who seem to "have it all." She starts each day anew, apparently convinced that life is grand!

> *"In her persists that primal innocence we are born with but fades away with the passage of time … and the living of life. In Abigayle you can see the pure joy we all let get away from us."*
> N'fa Ali Badara Mansaray

Ordinarily, you would think the fact that Abigayle is non-verbal would make her grumpy, as she usually can't express her needs and interests. She cannot tell me if she thinks her outfit is ugly or her hips are too big. She cannot share if she is ill or where something hurts. She cannot tell me that she is craving some special food or drink that is not in the house. Yes, she does have a tantrum when her high priority needs are not met, if she's given challenging demands or is not feeling well. However, she does not let her inability to communicate verbally define how she lives her day-to-day life.

For her, it's almost as if she does not realize that she has developmental differences. So, she doesn't know to be upset about them. She doesn't seem to see herself as a victim or perceive that she is missing out on anything. I think if she classified her differences as problems, it wouldn't change them. It would just make her overall experience worse. She relishes life—*if* she feels well and gets her way! She brings so much positivity into the world, which has taught me that my parents were right: it's all about perspective. Like Shakespeare wrote, "a rose by any other name would smell as sweet."

pure joy

Now Put the Lesson to Work in Your Own Life …

Lesson Learned:
Life is grand, if you don't know any better

I have learned that life is grand. Take a few minutes to consider the good around and within you.

Take an inventory of what is working for you in your life right now.

- Shift your thinking to the greatness all around you, and watch it multiply! It's key that we use the gifts and talents that are meant to create more greatness in our lives. Are you utilizing yours? If not, what can you do to utilize them?
- What parts of yourself do you need to refocus and rescue?
- What areas in your life need to be reinvented or evolved?

What are you letting get you down today? Refocus on good and positive thoughts and feelings. Let go of limited thinking and stressful thoughts.

- We can always find things and circumstances around us to stress about. If we do, the stresses will multiply until we really have something to worry about—like declining health. Don't let any of it get you down! You control more than you know. Reset for more!
- Every day, decide that you deserve to enjoy the day in front of you. The alternative is wasteful and dreary.
- Why not just decide that today is your day of greatness, no matter what is going on around you, what people are telling you, or what you are telling yourself? Just try one day of greatness where you don't let anyone or anything bring you down. At the end of that one day, ask yourself, "*What happened?*" Now, press REPEAT!

What are the childlike fantasies you let go of long ago that need to be rekindled?

- Without a dream, where will you end up? Take time to stretch your imagination and build your imaginative skills to create a better future for yourself and those you love.
- Are you surrounding yourself with "can do" people, or with people who don't have an imagination for a greater future for us all?
- Are you keeping an open mind to all the possibilities?
- Are you trying to prescribe your future with limited thinking?
- Understand that you don't have all the answers and knowledge that will inevitably exist in your future.
- Don't be your own daily invader of happiness!

Reminder: Life is grand, if you don't know any better

Life Lesson: You don't always get what you "think" you want or need, but it is important to embrace what you have.

After all, what you have may just be all that you need. Remember how thankful you felt when some prayers weren't answered, and some wishes didn't come true?

I laugh as I write this. I tell everyone that Abigayle is so cute that she could get away with murder (not literally, of course). Her precious little smile buys her a lot in the way of reprieves. I do spoil her with extra time on her golf cart or extra goodies if she flashes me a big smile. She is very persistent and obsessive in obtaining her highest priorities.

Abigayle gets a lot of grace, but she doesn't always get her way. While she does not understand *all* the words I say to her, she has always understood the word *no*. But, in true teenager fashion, she has recently appeared to tune out that word. Many times, the minute I start to walk in her direction to put a stop to whatever negative behavior she's engaged in, she stops doing it. She will look at me with a face that says, "I'm innocent and don't know what you are talking about, Mommy." She's testing me, just like any other teenager would. She is still in the learning phase of embracing her unmet desires.

Our family wants everything in the world for Abigayle. Since everything in the world is not attainable right now, we always try to find ways to focus on the blessings and make the most of what is within reach for her. We let go of what is out of our control and instead focus on the things we can do to make the most of the gifts she exhibits. We try to remember to focus on the blessings we have—not on what we don't have or cannot get from our relationship with her.

My family has accepted that Abigayle will likely never ride a bike, go to college, have a job, live independently, have a romantic relationship, or do any of the many other things her sister will likely get to enjoy in life. That being said, we still know that we are blessed in so many unique ways by having her in our lives. We are not victims of our circumstances. In the end, I also know that we could always have less, or things could be worse. For that, I am thankful.

I've never known anyone who has not been faced with some form of tragedy or heartbreak for some reason or another in their life. I do believe in miracles—I also know that God can change our more challenging circumstances, and I accept today for what it is and count my blessings. Life's little moments, both the good and the bad, are educational. I don't know about you, but most days I feel tired of learning the hard way, and I pray for the "good ole days" to return. Growing pains evidently never stop, but we can make the most of any circumstance.

Now Put the Lesson to Work in Your Own Life ...

Lesson Learned:
You don't always get what you "think" you want or
need, but it is important to embrace what you have

I have learned that our prayers aren't always answered the way we like, and we don't always get what we "think" is best for our lives. Take a few minutes to consider a new vision with new outcomes.

Were it not for Abigayle's autism, I would not live in the paradise of Florida or have my current amazing job. Her needs are what drove us to make decisions that led me to the place I never dreamed was available to me. By embracing Abigayle's challenges, a better life than we ever imagined opened up to us.

Count your blessings in life, which may be unanswered prayers, and wait for your silver lining to be revealed.

What is it that you are wanting in life but not receiving? What are all the possible reasons?

- Is there a growth opportunity you're missing out on because you are too busy looking at the situation as "bad" or too focused on what *isn't*, rather than what *is* helpful or what the experience can mean for your life?
- For me, my experience with Abigayle gives me an opportunity to serve—that may just be my ultimate and impactful purpose in life.
- What is your silver lining?
- What are you missing out on while you're looking at the "wrong" things? For instance, if I focused on the social media posts of my friends with their "perfect" houses, and instead obsessed over mine being messy, then I would miss out on the time I have with my children while we are making it beautifully messy. I would spend my time in areas that don't feed my soul—they drain it.

What and who are you holding on to from your past that no longer serves you?

- This could be as simple as carrying past rejections or mistakes on your shoulders.
- Is there a regret from your past that you are holding on to?
- Humans tend to look back on events with a skewed sense of reality. We try to hold people and events in a particular place as if nothing has evolved over time. So, are you holding onto something (or someone) that no longer exists outside of your mind and heart, and which no longer serves you or your future?
- We cannot truly hold on to things; we don't take anything with us when we die. What are you holding on to tightly even though it will disappear over time?
- **It is time to let go—because time itself has already done so!**

Are past failures impacting your future victories?

- Have you taken the failure to heart in a way that has stifled a passion project or caused you to shy away from taking on a new adventure?
- Remember, timing is key. We are all here for a purpose. Consider whether your attempt that ended in failure was just a stepping-stone toward a better use of your skills and passions.
- There are always multiple ways to get to the same place, so don't stop pressing forward with whatever is in your heart.

Reminder: You don't always get what you "think" you want or need, but it is important to embrace what you have

Life Lesson: Life is imperfect and out of your control, so you might as well keep moving forward

When I decided to start focusing on writing this book, I took three vacation days from work. I was ready to kick butt writing all day long, every day. I had this beautiful picture in mind of what this experience would be like. I was so excited. Then, life happened. Although I was on "vacation," I was still a mom, so I had my "mom duties" throughout the day. There is just no vacationing from that reality ... *my* reality.

The first day of writing went well. I felt like I'd accomplished enough to be satisfied. On the second day, Abigayle had a horrible rash. I kept her home from school and took her to the doctor. So, I lost one of the three days. On the third day, I woke up to Abigayle covered in vomit from a seizure she'd had during the night. Additionally, my phone was ringing off the hook with requests from colleagues and family. So, my idyllic time of writing did not turn out as I had envisioned and planned.

I could have responded by being upset, or I could have thrown a tantrum of my own—but then I realized that was *exactly* why I needed to get this book out there. I'm not the only one facing such challenges. There is so much outside of our control, and life never stops throwing challenges our way.

Making the Most of ... Everything!

100% attention and time must be devoted to Abigayle throughout the day, regardless of our own personal needs and desires for sleep, recreation, socializing, and more. Our family plans around Abigayle, which means managing her schedule, her golf cart obsession, her care needs (for instance: bathing, many outfit changes, brushing teeth, and pull-on diaper changes), nutritional needs, safety, and more. She will take small breaks here and there to watch animated movies on her iPad, but we cannot depend on her accepting a breaktime of our choosing from her golf cart rides—or at all.

The effort to watch and care for her is much more than is required for the typical teenager, meaning a lot of planning and negotiating schedules are among our many responsibilities. It often takes more than one person at a time to support some of Abigayle's care. I'm not complaining though, as I know many parents wish for more time with their children, while some people just wish to be blessed with children in the first place. Our situation *just is*, and we experience all that those developmental differences bring to our lives in the best way possible: by looking at the gifts we receive.

We spend many, many hours a day on the golf cart. Taking turns driving Abigayle around helps our backs recover from the many hours of sitting in place. I look at the time as an opportunity to cuddle and get in a good Audible book or music that feeds my soul. I share my experiences from those books with others who tell me they do not have time to read or listen to Audible. All that means is that they just don't prioritize it. I make the most of my time by creating a better life from what I learn, and by soaking up nature as we drive around in circles for hours a day.

Tiring and Trying Times Require Tenderness

The tantrums are numerous many days, but they are also fleeting. As I respond to the hands coming aggressively towards me in frustration during one of her tantrums, I find myself repeating, "It's okay, Abigayle. It is okay. You are going to be okay. It is going to be okay. You are okay." I *try* to stay in an emotionally loving state rather than responding angrily. I pull my energy down to a calm demeanor so as to not elevate the outburst. I find a way to protect myself and embrace her firmly, which can be calming to her when she gets overstimulated.

Don't get me wrong—there are tiring days, during which I screech when Abigayle kicks at another window or windshield. There are days when I am tired at the onset and the drink thrown across the room makes me scream, "ABIGAYLE!"—only to have her throw another drink minutes later while I am still cleaning up the first, all while dancing with her toes and spreading it everywhere.

Yes, I have my moments—just yesterday, as a matter of fact! Then, there are times like tonight when I have to yell out for reinforcements, which happens more and more as she has grown taller and stronger.

65

She straightens right up on most days when I call out for "DAD!" I just try to make those days with loud voices few and far between. Sometimes, I just have to laugh!

It's important to know that on the days when I am exhausted and/or stressed, it is much harder to manage the tantrums. On these days, it also seems like the volume and intensity of the tantrums increase. It's like she smells weakness and stress in our voices. This is why our self-care and support units are so important as caretakers.

Most importantly, I do not take it personally when she takes her frustrations out on me. I just go through the emotional moment without holding on to lingering emotions. Sometimes, I think I'm *too* good at staying unemotional to the negativity coming at me. On my good days, I'm unbothered, so much so that some look at me and think that I am enabling her bad behavior by my response or nonresponse. I have been trained that responding will drive her to do it more for the attention, but there are different theories as to how to manage her behaviors and these situations. I come from a place of love, as that is all I know.

When things start flying and hair gets pulled, I try not to feed the negative energy. It is my way of managing the situation, but I have sometimes seen others manage more effectively with a strong tone. I have experimented with using this tone, but I just don't have the commanding strength in my voice. When I get frustrated, Abigayle laughs at me. I just do my very best and move on ... allowing myself and Abigayle a little grace.

Logic Does Not Provide Certainty

God gave me the gifts of unconditional love and easy forgiveness. Unlike George and my mom, God did not gift me with a strong and authoritative tone. I use the gifts I have been given. I share this because we all need to feel good about how we respond to things in life and who we are. We all manage the best we can, even if *how we manage* may not be viewed as the best way. It may just be all we can do, and that's okay.

What seems logical to some regarding how to manage the tantrums may not seem logical to others, and what works some days does not work on other days. Heck, even what works for my husband or my mom does not work for me. It's always different being Mom, you know. Through the years, I've received conflicting advice from many experts. If *they* don't always know best, then I think I can have a great confidence in my own parental instincts, which are filtered through my knowledge of my own capabilities.

There is always great judgment that comes with parenting any child, so we just have to know ourselves and do the best that we can in our own shoes and with our own skills. I stay focused in the zone of maintaining love and safety. I try to disconnect both emotionally and physically as I manage through a crisis. Failure is only in the eye of the beholder! When it's all said and done, I just let go!

What Helps Me to Keep Going Forward

Taking care of ourselves the best way possible will help us be able to respond as life takes us down our winding, bumpy roads. I gain my control back on the tough days by reengaging in the things that make me happy (i.e., Hallmark movies, music, time with a friend, or a warm shower). It is also critical to rest and to find an outlet for my emotions. When I write, I feel a release of emotions, which balances me. On the days those tools don't do the trick, I decide that my circumstances won't control my experiences, and I turn to my faith.

Many people who know me think that I'm blessed with natural positivity. I so wish that were true; instead, I have to fight every day, decide to view things in a positive light, and look for blessings. The people around me have a great influence on my ability to stay positive or down in the dumps. I dare myself to CREATE happiness and positivity in my life and avoid negative influences. When I find it challenging to focus on the positive in my own life, I try to reach out to others to have a positive influence on their day. This effort of sharing goodness and love with others feeds my soul and ricochets the good feelings back to me.

Yes, I have tons of opportunities to wallow in pity and focus on the negatives. I have more than one acquaintance who has told me they feel like they are in jail as a parent of a child with developmental differences. I know I could give in and give up on the hard days. It can be really hard, but I cannot keep my focus there. I am what doctors have called a "warrior mom," but I give myself lots of pampering to stay balanced with my own needs. If I let the negativity pile onto me, it would certainly bury me. That's why I always redirect towards the positive when I start to feel the downward pull.

It would be easy for me to justify having a bad attitude, or to pity my own circumstances. I choose every day to have the perspective that life is worth experiencing, and I must rise to the challenge. I carry faith, on the bad days, that there is a silver lining and that things will balance out for my good in the end. I try to wake up expecting miracles, and I ask myself, "What miracle will come my way today?" Sometimes, I get in a funk and fail, but that rarely happens.

Usually, the funk is caused by those with whom I have chosen to surround myself—not the impact of autism. That should really make you think about those you choose to spend your time with. Are you making decisions that make your life harder or easier?

> *"Can any one of you by worrying add*
> *a single hour to your life?"*
> Matthew 6:27 (NIV)

When Your Already-Challenging World Gets Turned Upside Down

I am now writing during the COVID-19 pandemic. My family, like many others, does not have our regular childcare available. For many months, we did not have any of Abigayle's therapy sessions, which are critical for her. Her public school was not in session onsite, but the school had hoped that we would join their Zoom calls while managing our work and caring for our very active Abigayle. These expectations came from a school where we received almost weekly calls from the Principal and Sheriff that we needed to pick up Abigayle due to a crisis (meaning they lost control of her). I could write a book specifically on our experiences attending this school.

Abigayle displayed challenging behaviors at the public school for some time, but she has been thriving since being home due to COVID. She was not able to tell me she was unhappy at the school, but the forced change of circumstances revealed it to me. Fortunately, after many months without support, we finally have Abigayle in an excellent therapy program and school. She is flourishing beyond anything our family has ever experienced.

Every day now starts and ends with a smile on her face, which warms my heart. No one has ever worked harder for Abigayle's needs than South Walton Academy in Santa Rosa Beach, Florida. In fact, due to her many requirements and complexities, many schools have turned us away immediately, or after being waitlisted for several years. I cannot wait to see her progress over time from working with these dedicated and experienced professionals. Her tantrums have already dramatically decreased, and her incredible ability to redirect from them has astounded us.

Love and Loss

While writing this book, my dad passed away unexpectedly after a lengthy and complex illness. When the darkness of death knocked on the door and took my dad, I looked for and found peace in my blessings. It was an incredible reminder of what is and what is not important in life and death. I am still charging forward to reach my goals. It looks a little different and is taking longer than originally envisioned, but I am moving forward. The key is to keep going!

> *"Therefore do not worry about tomorrow,*
> *for tomorrow will worry about itself. Each*
> *day has enough trouble of its own."*
> Matthew 6:34 (NIV)

Within the last year of my writing this, besides losing my father and an almost fatal car accident for my young nephew, there has been so much more strife and loss around me. My younger brother, only in his mid-40s, had a massive stroke. How can this happen? Because of his young age, he is the last person in the family I would ever be concerned about this happening to. He and his lovely family are holding on strong, but they are still in the early days as I write this.

Be Your Own Role Model in Living Life Like a Champion

Many times, I have prayed for a day of relief, a week, a moment—*something*. Knowing life does not always comply with all my wishes and prayers, I recognize the value of just rolling with it and not letting the little disruptions turn into larger issues or ruin any of my few days left on earth. I try to stop focusing on all the little things that challenge my day, especially those events I won't even remember in a few years (or maybe even in five minutes) if I am lucky enough to be here. Tantrums and violent attacks can be traumatic in the moment, but once they are over, I have to move forward. I don't have time to waste. Do you?

If I'd let those disruptions stop me from writing, you would not be reading this right now. I have decided to be my own role model and to live like a champion so that my life will be full of joy and sunshine, rather than it just being something I endure. I keep fighting for my happiness. I am my own champion. I do the best I can and feel confident that my decisions are exactly what I am supposed to do or accomplish.

Now Put the Lesson to Work in Your Own Life ...

Lesson Learned:
Life is imperfect and out of your control, so you
might as well keep moving forward

I have learned there is much that I cannot control in life, so I might as well enjoy it. Take a few minutes to consider the areas in your life where you need to let go or take charge.

Some days can feel like you're at the beach and the waves keep coming at you, almost knocking you off your feet. The first wave may be lack of sleep; the second, financial burdens of caring for a child with developmental differences; the third, a violent tantrum ... after that, they just keep coming. These waves are hard on anyone, which is important to recognize and *feel* before taking your control back.

Life will keep coming at us. We must take the example from others that everything can change in an instant. Some changes are based upon our choices, while others are impacted by the choices of others. Either way, we all experience life's tragedies. We can only do what is within our control.

Sometimes, just moving forward is good enough—no matter the pace!

- In my world, life is experienced better with hope and faith in goodness over the darkness that tries to invade my days. Stay focused on love and faith, no matter the little life invaders of the moment. This day will pass one way or another, so it might as well be as good as you can make it.
- Knowing I cannot do it all alone, I surround myself with wonderful family members and friends I can lean on to help keep my spirits up, some of whom even jump in during the tough times. The best way to cultivate these relationships is to be a friend on whom others can lean first.
  - With whom have you surrounded yourself?
  - Who are you serving?

Start with God!

- Too many of my friends and family go around in circles stressing and worrying about how "they" will fix a problem. When the problems are big and out of control, I turn to God before I start with myself. I don't try and fail multiple times before giving up or giving it to God. I start with God first, then I do my part based upon inspiration within.
- Our imagination has limits, and it's not big enough to create all the known solutions to a problem. Listen within after you turn it over to God. The answer will come to you. The road may be bumpy and winding, but in the end it will be for your good—whether it feels that way or not! Trust is key—trust in God and in yourself.
- Wait and watch for your silver lining to be revealed! Life is full of surprises just around the corner. Do your job, and then trust for your prayers to be heard and answered.

Take care of yourself, because no one else can like you can!

- We must protect our minds, hearts, and bodies. Yes, others can help, but it takes action to preserve ourselves at our best.
- Put time into developing disciplines for a better life. Make a list now. Yes, you know what you need to do, so go make it happen.
- Take it off the "to-do" list by creating new routine habits today for a better tomorrow! Yes, that will mean hard work and rearranging your schedule, but just think how great you will look and feel at that next in-person function!

Reminder: Life is imperfect and out of your control, so you might as well keep moving forward

CHAPTER 7

"HERE AND NOW" MATTERS MOST

W ITH AUTISM, YOU never really know what is in your future or when a crisis may arise. So, you must take every moment in stride. I hear so many parents worrying about things with their children. As for me, I am just happy when a day goes by without a huge crisis!

Life Lesson: Focus on high priority and greatest impact

Abigayle, being non-verbal, does not clearly communicate every need she has, so we've learned to be tuned in to her. When she has a high-priority need, she will find a way to break through and let us know by showing or leading us to what she wants. Since such communication is rare, we know we'd better pay attention when it occurs. She knows how to focus, and she obsessively goes after her highest priority needs, which is very effective. If we don't respond appropriately, a tantrum will ensue.

I've also learned how to prioritize my own needs and include only activities that have the greatest impact on my limited resources—both in time and money. Since Abigayle requires increased 24/7 care, George and I must be choosy with how we spend our moments. To have any time to myself at all, I have to get up early and go to bed late. I don't spend a lot of time on low-impact efforts, as time for myself and our family is limited.

I have listened to people say, "Why don't you just … do this or that?" and tell me that they know they could "fix" my child if they had the time. I know I could do some things differently that might make my life better in the future (if I had time). I know this, but sometimes

I just don't have it in me to absorb the short-term costs for the changes needed, especially without more help.

I am not a perfect person or mom, but I do my very best. No one could love Abigayle more than I do. She is my angel on earth. I know that doing my best is enough for her and for our family, so that is what I do—my very best. When that's not enough, I have learned to allow help from others.

I forgive myself for what I cannot do for myself and the household, as I will always prioritize parenting and safety. Everything else will just have to be the way it is until another day and time when things change. If someone does not like it or wants to judge, I would ask who and what their priorities are. People always ask me how I manage everything I do. I tell them that we all have 24 hours in a day. It all comes down to choices and priorities.

Now Put the Lesson to Work in Your Own Life ...

Lesson Learned:
Focus on high priority and greatest impact

I have to change my ways and focus on high priority for the greatest impact. Take a few minutes to evaluate what changes need to be made in your life, then rank them according to your defined priorities.

If you focus on high-priority needs with high impact, you may be surprised by what you can accomplish and what you can avoid. Maybe you're someone who has a lot of time on your hands—that doesn't mean you have time to waste. Whether your time is limited or plentiful, use your resources when you need them the most, and conserve your energy when you can.

What is important to you? Does the time you spend each day reflect those priorities?

- Too often, our greatest priorities are the last thing that we make time to focus on, despite always being at the top of our "to-do" list.
- Ongoing learning of any kind should be a top priority to keep you ahead of the rest. No matter what you do with your days and career ... do it to the best of your abilities!

What changes do you need to prioritize to improve for the better?

- Are you taking care of yourself for the value of the treasure you are to this world?
- Is it time to make a change in some key area of your life that you have been putting off? What is distracting you? What are you ignoring? What no longer serves you?
- What are your weaknesses? Create a list about what you can do about them. For instance, are there skill sets that you can obtain to make you grow professionally in order to get promoted or get a fulfilling new job?

- How are you wasting precious time that you could be using to be more productive towards your goals? Heck, what *are* your goals? Do you have any? Have they been updated?
- Are you using all your key resources to make your life the best it can be?
  - Are you exercising for mental and physical wellbeing?
  - Are you journaling for clarity and to bring forward new ideas? It only takes a phone or piece of paper.
  - Are you getting the proper rest (during the best hours for quality sleep) on a consistent basis? Are you aligned with your circadian rhythms?
  - Are you surrounding yourself with the right people?

Reminder: Focus on high priority and greatest impact

Life Lesson: It is not what we go through in a day that can drain us, but what our *mind* goes through in a day ...

No exhaustion is as tiring to me as mental and emotional exhaustion. With autism, you have to be "on" every second of the day, as every second has an opportunity to erupt into a very dangerous or harmful situation. Abigayle may be having the best day ever, but my mind cannot relax until the day ends successfully. It seems every time I brag on her, a huge tantrum follows.

Tantrums are a risk, but dangers can also enter our world under the most bizarre circumstances. Dangers and triggers for tantrums are plentiful and can happen without warning. This leads to always being on watch—like a lifeguard, George and I are on duty 24/7, even on a calm and gorgeous day. The calm means nothing when compared to the risk. If we let it, this constant attention to watching for and anticipating danger can be a huge strain on our energy, health, and overall quality of life. Living on watch can create increased stress that can get out of control if we don't control our thinking.

I take life one day at a time, and I live each day comforted by the fact that I am here to do my part in life to serve. I'm not here to live *for* others or worry about what they do. I do the best job that I can, and I let the rest go. I give what I can but protect myself and my limits in a way that no one else will do for me. I have often been told that one failing of mine is that I make difficult things look too easy, so it makes people think whatever I'm going through isn't that challenging. This can make people misconstrue my struggles and not be able to identify when I need support, especially if I'm not asking for it. Knowing this helps me elevate my self-awareness—which is key to my survival.

> *"If you cannot do great things, do*
> *small things in a great way."*
> Napoleon Hill

"I can do all things through Him
who strengthens me." (ESV)

It is all in my thinking ...

My life has some limits on what I can do in many areas, and there are a ton of extra costs involved in caring for a child with multiple disabilities. When I think of Abigayle's future, when I am no longer on this earth ... well, let's just say that it's a hard thought to handle. The thought alone could really bring me down if I wanted to let it control my emotions. I have plenty of worries regarding our future care with Abigayle as we age, too. I could dwell on all of the "what ifs?" that could go wrong in Abigayle's day ...

Will she run away from a teacher and into the street today?

Will Abigayle steal another kid's peanut snack and have another allergic reaction?

Will she sleep tonight?

Will she get kicked out of school?

I think you get the point ... I could make my existence on earth a living hell if I chose to let things fester and focused on everything that could be construed as "bad" in my life. Don't get me wrong, I have spent many hours worrying about things. What I've learned from those hours is that worry does not do any good; it just steals my precious moments. The things that have caused me sleepless nights were a breeze to go through. Yet, the things that really rocked my world are typically not things that I have spent time worrying about or anticipating. Isn't this true of everyone's tragedies ... the gut-wrenching, life-changing moments that change us forever are typically never anticipated?

At one point, Abigayle needed to have a test done that required many, many wires being attached to her scalp for multiple days. I thought, "There's no way she will allow those things to be attached to her for days. She'll get strangled in her sleep by the wires." So, I stayed with her overnight to manage it all.

Well, she always finds ways to get through the tough tests and trying times like a champion, and usually without any hiccups. God always comes through for us and makes these most concerning of times pass more easily than I'd feared. I continually remind myself of this every time doubt and worry seep into my brain. The tougher the situation, the more comfort and knowing I have that all will turn out better than I can imagine. It always does. I can count on it!

Dangers Within

As I've mentioned, Abigayle does not understand danger. She's a thrill seeker. It seems every day there is something that could end up badly. Common everyday items can become dangerous around Abigayle in ways that are unforeseen. In fact, once we had to take Abigayle for stitches in the emergency room—a story in itself—because she stepped onto a doll stroller that slid forward, causing an accident during her time at a childcare facility. One doctor told us Abigayle would require anesthesia to get stitches, but another doctor later saved the day with solutions that would avoid it. It was a long day, but we made it through.

She is an "eloper," which is just a fancier way of saying she loves to run away. She is very, very fast too! Usually, if you are looking at her, you can see it in her face right before she takes off. She will run at any time, for any reason or no reason at all, usually while laughing for making you chase her. She could run into a street in front of a car without a worry in the world. This alone could make me live in a state of constant worry, but I cannot allow these thoughts to dominate me.

In our house, we tell everyone we are under lockdown because Abigayle does not have a healthy relationship with water. She obsesses over it, so she is not cautious around it (except around the pool). She can also tolerate pain in a different and extreme way, so we lock all bathroom doors at all times of the day for her safety. She would stand in toilets or burn herself with hot water if we did not. People have told me that they could not live this way. For us, it's just life. We accept what it is. We cannot dwell in dreams of other circumstances.

I could focus on the negative and make those thoughts multiply. I could allow myself to stay in a dark place of worry and dread. Instead,

I find ways to celebrate Abigayle's progress and be grateful for what we have (for example, she is affectionate). I can turn those limits into gifts, as it is all in how we perceive things to be. Since we cannot do a lot of things that other families do, we stay close to home. That has its own advantages, which I think will pay dividends for years to come.

> ***We cannot cry over spilled milk—that mishap
> is a common occurrence in our house!***

Natalie has seen acquaintances being dramatic or stressing about the silliest things. She shares how blessed she is to have the experiences she does because she knows what really matters and when to let things go. If she worried about all the little things that happen in a day in the life of a family with a child diagnosed with autism, she would go crazy or be very depressed. She sees the difference between frustrations that should be fleeting and real-life worries that deserve her attention and resources. In this sense, Natalie has learned important life lessons that elude some adults for decades.

I Let It Go

Mothers are always expected to keep it all together. On the days where I am tense or under extreme pressure, I take a shower and let it all out in private. The shower itself is therapeutic, but there is also no evidence of the tears ... the sight of which might make me even sadder for so many reasons. I may become sadder that I'm in a situation that causes tears, sadder that I did not have the control that I wanted, or sadder for taking it all alone at times. The shower can be a great refuge.

I am a firm believer that you have to get it all out of your system or it will kill you over time. During some stressful occasions, the shower becomes my sanctuary. I use it as a trigger to try to get the tears out, but it does not always work. I cannot always count on time for a quality shower. In these cases, I turn to my support units and other techniques sprinkled throughout this book to release the negative energy. It doesn't matter how we get our release, but what is important is that we release the negative energy in a way that works for our bodies, our circumstances, and otherwise.

If I cannot change the situation, I change how I look at it. I don't always think of this right away, but it will eventually become the only solution. This is incredibly effective for dealing with any of life's problems. There is so much outside of our control, and dwelling on our problems will not solve them.

I'm so thankful for being blessed with the ability to choose to let things go. When Abigayle has a tantrum that leaves me feeling like I've been in some sort of fight club, the last thought associated with it occurs the *second* the event is over. All my life, I've been told that I can let things go too easily. A caring boss once told me that my tendency to let things go could be misconstrued by the perpetrator of an offense, who might think it was not as bad as it really was, given my lack of a sustained response. I guess it's true, but I cannot hold in the bad energy. My body repels it, just like it would any other foreign object.

Unfortunately, there are those times of sustained impact or repeated efforts to drag me down. During those times, I look within for the answer. I consider what my part is in the ongoing tragedy of the day and how I can impact it. For instance, if I recognize the trigger for the outburst, I consider what I can do to avoid it in the future. If my actions and changes do not provide the answer, I try to find a more positive way of looking at the problem.

> *Any negative encounter in our life should be released as it relates to the pain, but it can still be remembered for the lessons that help shape us.*

I could hold on to anger every time I see the scratches, scars, scabs, bruises, lumps of pulled-out hair on the floor, or any other damage from the tantrums. I could carry that anger into my relationship with Abigayle or with the rest of the family or people I encounter. It would be so easy to become the victim, but I would get nothing for it aside from the remaining negativity. Instead, I try to create a loving and giving environment in the hopes that these traits will compound.

Darkness and evil beyond our imagination can exist around us, but it does not have to dwell within us. I do what I can to create brightness in the darkness. Then, I turn to God to carry my family and other loved ones through it.

> *Everyone is in pain and has shame for one thing or another, so we should all identify with the commonality of the struggle and respond with love and patience for one another.*

Backbone of Faith

Everyone has a role in their family where strength is needed. In the hard times, I turn to my faith for strength, protection, and healing. The pain that life can bring does not allow for any answers other than those communicated through faith. I understand the value of being a force of faith to help myself and my family to endure through the hard times.

Now Put the Lesson to Work in Your Own Life ...

Lesson Learned:
It is not what we go through in a day that can drain
us, but what our *mind* goes through in a day ...

I've learned to watch my thoughts. Have you?

Take a few minutes to discover how to get more out of life by following
your rightful path—the one that energizes you.

*What's on your mind today that needs to be released? Let's talk about
how to replace it!*

- Take a walk today (in nature, if possible) and think about how
  you are spending your thoughts and the impact that they have
  on you. Are you keeping your mind on the right things?
- Consider what changes you need to make regarding who
  you spend your most precious resource—time—on. We're all
  living for just a quick blink of time– don't forget that!
- Are you surrounding yourself and spending your time with
  those who bring you the most joy? Do those people help
  advance you to greater heights? We should all be very picky
  in how and with whom we spend our time!

*It's so important to be aware of what you are paying attention to at
every moment. Is it positive and inspiring—which will GIVE you endless
energy—or is it negative and demotivating, draining your energy?*

- Where you put your thoughts will impact how much energy
  you have reserved when you need it.

*Reminder: It is not what we go through in a day that can drain us, but
what our mind goes through in a day ...*

Life Lesson: Planning is pertinent

I'll be the first to tell you: I love, love, love my planner, to-do lists, spreadsheets, and running future scenarios in my mind (most of which never come to fruition). I love to map everything out, but I never expect the plans to work out as envisioned. I'm flexible and go with what comes. Then I plan AGAIN!

With Abigayle, I cannot do anything without major creative planning, whether she is part of the plan to go somewhere or left at home. Very few people will stay with Abigayle alone ... I can count them on one hand. So, careful and meticulous planning goes into scheduling for each workday and every single time I leave the house, as well as every time I have something I need to do that does not include riding Abigayle around on the golf cart. For instance, if Abigayle is to join us for a dinner at a restaurant or otherwise, I must anticipate her walking in and right back out or throwing a major tantrum in public.

Then, there was yesterday, when she refused to walk in the grocery store on the first try. We were only successful on getting our groceries after an initial delay on the *second* try. So, backup plans for all situations are a must.

Surprises in Life

Planning is great, but Abigayle is still unpredictable. She may be fine going out to eat in restaurants for weeks, but then we'll take her in one and she'll immediately throw herself to the ground screaming, pulling her hair, biting her wrists, and kicking her feet. She may do this without any warning, despite our family's best efforts to consider her mood for the day, making sure she is not hangry, ensuring she is hungry enough to sit through the eating process (rarely will she sit for the duration), and considering how her skin has been lately (another aggravator). We have tried to go out to lunch for holidays, including Mother's Day, and she refused to even step one foot in the restaurant. Of course, there are other times where we enjoy a fabulous meal together as a family—those days make it all worth it.

What Will Happen Tomorrow Cannot Rule the Day

While it's nice to think ahead, there is some planning that is critical to my family's ability to preserve our future. My biggest concern with Abigayle is what will happen when my husband and I are no longer on this earth. Knowing it is hard to find care and that we are aging, we have to plan for a time when we are not physically fit to manage the demands of chasing Abigayle when she runs off or protecting ourselves from a tantrum—plus all the other physical demands of providing her self-care, some of which she resists. I hope none of these events happen soon, but I cannot be lax in my planning.

I know Natalie will be a tremendous provider for Abigayle. Now that we are getting closer to the twins turning 18, Natalie will play a big role in the planning. However, I want her to also be able to live the life that she intends, including having a family of her own. While she will be part of the solution, I want Natalie to have wonderful options for Abigayle's care as an adult. This is why I plan to find, support, or build my own care adult center where I can be assured caretakers are vetted. With Abigayle being non-verbal and quite active, as well as having self-injurious and challenging behaviors, the stakes are high for us to make sure that she gets just the right care from just the right people.

> **"It takes as much energy to wish as it does to plan."**
> Eleanor Roosevelt

The uncertainty of the future alone could drag down my energy on any given day, but I know that I cannot focus negatively on the future. I must rely on my faith and my past experiences that everything will always work out over time. I'll make my plans and will not live in fear and dread for the future, one that certainly won't show up exactly as I envision. Who knows what Abigayle will achieve in the future? I will research, plan, and take inspired action. This is all that I can do before I have to let it all go.

I share all of this as a reminder that we cannot prepare ourselves for everything. If we try to prepare ourselves for everything, we might just miss out on other treasures in life. We cannot avoid going out around town completely because we are scared of what "might" happen. If we did, we would miss out on the good times altogether, as anything "might" happen at any moment ... in Abigayle's life as well as yours or mine.

During the times when Abigayle would not sit through a meal, she and I would hang out in the car or drive around. We would have our own personal time and George would get that rare one-on-one time with Natalie to catch up on her life. Things may not go as we planned, but that doesn't mean they aren't going exactly according to a *bigger* plan for a better life—one that threads through all our time on this earth and beyond.

As a result of Abigayle's unpredictability, I work to be prepared for the unexpected. I go with the flow, and I continually have opportunities in front of me to maintain and grow my flexibility muscles in order to make the most of my moments. Some surprises in life are good (and some not so good), but in the end all the events in our lives work towards something that is good. We just need to look around sometimes to find the good around us.

> *"Whoever seeks good finds favor, but evil*
> *comes to one who searches for it."*
> Proverbs 11:27 (NIV)

Now Put the Lesson to Work in Your Own Life ...

Lesson Learned:
Planning is pertinent

I have learned that planning goes a long way in reducing my stress and worry for what the future holds. We cannot control our future, but we can work to mitigate some of the more challenging events that we can foresee.

What are you looking to in your future that you need to put in the right perspective, plan, and then let go to live for today?

What are some things that you have been putting off that seem too big for you to manage today, but which can come back to bite you (or the ones you love) if you are unprepared?

- Think about whether you are properly set up for your retirement. Do you need to make changes today?
- Do you have a will, power of attorney (POA), and advanced directive (POA for medical directives)?
- Do you have life insurance and burial insurance or plans? Have you shared your important documents and passwords with your loved ones?
- We never know how much time we have. It's key that we create the best outcomes for the future by planning where we can today.

What signs are you seeing or what nudges are you getting to make changes in your life?

- We all get little sparks of energy here and there telling us to create something new for our lives. Are you listening to the little whispers or responding to the little nudges? What has been nudging you lately?

- There is not just one path to any goal. If you have a roadblock in one area, create a new pathway. You never know where it might lead you.
- Most importantly, move forward with inspired action. Do not stay stuck!
- Without action, you will still be in this same place this time next month or next year ... only wishing and waiting for change to find you. You deserve more! Make your future happen by starting today!
- Buy a beautiful journal and perfectly smooth pen that makes you feel good. Then, take time in nature and write down one priority goal. Once you have your priority goal, start creating the steps and timelines to achieve the future of your dreams. They are within your reach—all you have to do is act now!

Reminder: Planning is pertinent

Life Lesson: It is critical to develop and maintain faith and trust within yourself

If you approached me before I was a parent and asked me to parent a child similar to Abigayle, I would have told you that I don't have the capabilities necessary to do a good job. I would not have believed that I could be the mom that I am, or that I would be able to endure the things I've endured in our medical, mental, and physical journey with Abigayle. I would not have trusted that I have what it takes or have had the faith in myself that I could sustain and persevere. Yet, I now have the proof that I would have been wrong, and I CAN do it! I AM doing it!

There were so many times when I doubted my own capabilities and would have been incredibly wrong. I remember when I heard that I was having twins. I was so scared of failing. I didn't feel prepared, so I read a ton of material ... just enough to give me tremendous anxiety and tell my husband to throw out the books! Then there was the time when Abigayle got her feeding tube. The doctor explained it all to me, and I thought, "I can't do this. I'm going to get sick!" However, I did it very, very well within a day of starting it! We are all capable of so much more than we give ourselves credit. Without these challenging moments, I would never have known all of my capabilities and capacity.

When I hear the stories I tell others, about what I've gone through and go through each day, I cannot believe it. It sounds so much harder to me than it feels, but I also feel pain inside when I think of others going through the same. For me, it has been my reality from the day of their birth, so I don't know the difference of what I manage as a mom versus another mom without the increased demands. I don't give myself the credit that I deserve for the strength and power of my love. I just do what it takes, and it all seems to work out on its own. Well, according to God's perfect plan, that is.

Listen to Your Intuition ...

Early on, I discovered the tremendous value of my voice within. One story really sticks out from the early days, right after getting home from the NICU for the second time. We were excited to be home for a few days from NICU, but Abigayle's hospital days were not over yet. She started crying, kicking, scratching, and screaming all day long. She would fall asleep from exhaustion, but I knew something was very wrong. At one point, I was even told Abigayle had colic. Since Natalie had colic, I knew this was different. Something was very wrong.

Abigayle's known conditions (at the time) were already complicated, so the emergency room checked her into the hospital. After a spinal tap and every other test they could think of running, the doctor changed her food and was convinced that would solve the issue. She stayed close to a week, and the doctors assured me everything was okay. I sat in front of the doctor as she shared that they were about to let Abigayle go home. Tears started falling from my eyes. The tears were not because of the communication from the doctor, but from her lack of listening to the expert ... in this case, Abigayle's mom.

As the tears flowed, I was told "You're just tired." The doctor said all my hours at the hospital were taking a toll on me. It was implied that I was not thinking clearly and that all was fine with Abigayle. This was a teaching hospital with a great reputation, but this particular doctor would not listen to me. She actually sent Abigayle to "special care" and sent me home. She told me I needed sleep. With Abigayle in special care, I could no longer stay with her during her very painful state. I had to leave my preemie baby all alone in the hospital, without any relief or comfort. I shared with the doctor that no matter how tired I was at the time, I KNEW my child, and something was very wrong. This comment fell on deaf ears.

I called my pediatrician, who was not surprised, as she had been told of how this doctor had not listened to other parents. This didn't appease me. After a short stay in special care, Abigayle was released back into my care without any change in her behavior. Within a day, I was changing Abigayle's diaper when I noticed bulges in her lower abdomen. I was instructed to go right back to the hospital, where I was told I had discovered inguinal hernias. In that moment, I realized they never examined Abigayle's body ... even with all those invasive tests.

I saw the doctor who had previously refused to listen to my concerns about Abigayle. She mentioned she was surprised to see us back—but *I* wasn't surprised to be back. I told her I'd discovered what had been wrong with Abigayle this entire time. At least then she knew I had not been dreaming things up because of my lack of sleep, and it was most certainly not colic. I hope she remembered the experience when talking with other parents of her future patients.

The diagnosis was much more dire than colic. We were told Abigayle would likely not make it through a surgery to fix her hernias in her frail condition. It was too risky, so instead we had to keep managing the hernias. This involved emergency room visits on holidays and some great pain for Abigayle until she grew to a more stable condition, at which point the surgery was completed. Within days of the surgery, we saw a smile on Abigayle's face for the first time.

I cannot explain in words how I felt when she first smiled at me. It warmed my heart, but it was so much more than that after months and months of screaming from her pain! I'm so thankful this was before the time of COVID, because I had the ability to go in and out of the hospital to be with Natalie. I didn't have the concerns that parents today in similar situations are having to endure. I am so grateful for the gift of intuition and patience to make it through that difficult time. I came out stronger on the other side of it!

LISTEN to YOUR INTUITION!!! Many times, if not all, YOU do know best!

> *"Truly I tell you, if you have faith as small as*
> *a mustard seed, you can say to this mountain,*
> *'Move from here to there,' and it will move.*
> *Nothing will be impossible for you."*
> Matthew 17:20 (NIV)

Now Put the Lesson to Work in Your Own Life ...

Lesson Learned:
It is critical to develop and maintain faith and trust within yourself

I have learned the importance of developing and maintaining faith and trust within myself and God.

Take a few minutes to consider where you are falling short in providing a fair self-evaluation of who you are, how you contribute to this world, and the value of your legacy.

What is it that you should give yourself credit for—either for today or from the past? How can you trust that you can persevere under challenging circumstances?

- Everyone has doubts ... just don't let them be debilitating.
- Ask yourself, why not you?
- Why would others deserve what you will not give to yourself?
- Remember, you were divinely created for a purpose, and God will give you all that you need in order to fulfill it. It is not all on you. Strength is within you, whether you feel it now or not. Dig deep inside and you will find a reservoir of all that you need.

> **"You were designed for accomplishment, engineered for success, and endowed with the seeds of greatness."**
> Zig Ziglar

Your "Made It" Vision for Your Life

Envision your wildest dream and you succeeding ... what does it look like?

What does abundance in your life look like to you?

93

Picture yourself after you have "made it" to that next phase you are entering in life.

- ○ Where are you?
- ○ What are you doing?
- ○ How do you feel?
- ○ What do you see and smell, if anything?
- ○ What do you look like? How are you dressed?
- ○ What and who are you around?

This is your new goal and future reality. In order to achieve it, you must experience your "Made It" Vision for your life daily within your mind until it is a reality. Every time you can think of it in a day, think of your abundance and this snapshot of your new future reality.

For me, I have created a vision in my mind without mapping the course of what was to be my next career step. Twice now, I have been spot-on in my vision for the future prior to even knowing what would get me there. I asked myself, "*What does abundance look like for me?*" The picture that appeared in my mind so vividly actually became my reality ... twice! The "Made It" Vision led to the changes I made in my career, not the other way around.

Reminder: It is critical to develop and maintain faith and trust within yourself

EXTERNAL INFLUENCES ARE ON THE OUTSIDE ... KEEP THEM THERE

THERE IS A lot in our environment that could harm us, so it's important to filter what we internalize and who we allow to impact our internal world.

Life Lesson: There is a lot of noise around. Block it out!

For as long as I can remember, Abigayle has had an incredible ability to tune out the rest of the world (my husband can do the same when he wishes). But sometimes, she gets overwhelmed with ambient noise and cannot tune it out. At those times, she uses special earmuffs to block the sensory input. She knows that too much noise, certain noises, or noise that comes in from all directions, is disastrous.

I've also learned to block out the noise of life in order to have a peaceful day. Abigayle makes many noises, and I watch out for the ones I know are important. If I focused on all of them, I might go crazy during her stemming moments (repetitive or unusual noises or movements) of pressing the recorded book one hundred times, listening to the same movie one thousand times, or noisily shaking cups of ice.

"The world is full of noise. And finding quiet isn't about pushing everything out. It's just about pulling yourself in."
Victoria Schwab

Now Put the Lesson to Work in Your Own Life ...

Lesson Learned:
There is a lot of noise around. Block it out!

I have learned to tune out the news that does not nurture and feed my soul. Take a few minutes to create *more* in your life ... whatever that looks like for you.

What distractions or noise do you need to block out in order to create a better existence for yourself?

What noise is going on in your head that does not serve you?

What unkind things are you thinking about regularly that only make you feel worse in multiple areas of your life, or which otherwise create unnecessary anxiety?

The world can throw a lot at you. Be selective as to what you let penetrate your mind. You should have a filter for any incoming noise. Don't just react to everything that comes into your world; it can be overwhelming. Take time for yourself, daily or weekly, in a quiet place to think. Be very picky regarding what you let in your mind and life. Put your "earmuffs" on from time to time.

It is so important to have some "me time" and "quiet time"—yet so few take advantage of the opportunity to get up early or go to bed late to get it. There are ways to create time for yourself to think. Whether you are intentional about listening to your internal thoughts will either make or break your life. Take time today to tune out, or tune in, deliberately!

Reminder: There is a lot of noise around. Block it out!

Life Lesson: Dismiss the judgment of others as ignorance

Extraneous noise isn't the only thing that needs blocking; the critical judgment of others requires a strong filter as well. This is a lesson I had to teach Natalie early in life after she came to me upset with a friend over Abigayle. Natalie and the friend were playing, and her friend really wanted to play with a toy, but before touching it, she asked Natalie if Abigayle had "touched" the toy. After hearing Abigayle *had* touched it, the friend wouldn't play with the toy.

After that, Natalie was sensitive and protective of Abigayle with her friends. I explained to Natalie that judgment is about the person who judges, not about the subject of the judgment. Even with the lessons, right or wrong, that experience has always impacted subsequent interactions of Natalie introducing Abigayle to her friends.

> **"Walk with me for a while, my friend—you in my shoes, I in yours—and then let us talk."**
> Richelle E. Goodrich

Many times, sitters have been horrified by the treatment they have received from strangers while taking Abigayle on her outings. I'm grateful that Abigayle never seems to notice people staring at her. Staring can be very natural when people see things that appear to be different, but sometimes the stares of others can make people feel judged, uncomfortable, and insecure. Abigayle primarily stays in her own little world. She has always been happy in her environment, regardless of the reactions of others.

Abigayle still doesn't seem impacted by the pity (and sometimes disgust) carved onto the faces of bystanders as she tries to bite me or pull me to the ground in public. She just rolls through life with whatever attitude she has chosen for the day. Although Abigayle doesn't fully understand the judgment emanating from others, she can *feel* the energy around her, and she responds to it in a mirroring fashion. Unlike most of us, however, she does not allow other people's opinions to impact her own. We can all decide how much, and when, we let others' opinions impact our sense of self. Too often, we give power to others that they don't deserve.

"Be curious, not judgmental."
Walt Whitman

A few people over the years have told me that Abigayle could *learn* more and *do* more if we were parenting her *their* way. Many times, these people did not even know Abigayle or our family very well, but felt they knew what was best for her. I won't lie, it sometimes hurts when people imply or act as if I am not doing a *good enough* or *smart* job as a mom (the most important job I will ever have). What's worse is when they imply I am holding Abigayle back with my loving approach. Some like to judge us from the sidelines about Abigayle's behaviors and abilities based upon how George and I have chosen to parent—with a focus on love.

It is far too easy for others to judge from the outside without all the pressures from what her diagnosis brings to our family. The people full of judgment are not under the same non-stop stress of always striving to maintain control in a world with parts so far removed from any semblance of it. Yes, we all have our own stressors in life, but no other person on this earth has what I have within me and my experiences. They don't know what it's like for my family. They can only peer into our lives from the outside. When my family is judged for how we overcome our mountainous obstacles, I just remind myself that it was not my choice to give Abigayle to me. It was God's choice, and GOD KNOWS BEST!

God gave Abigayle her tribe ... her parents, sister, grandparents, aunts, uncles, loving caretakers, very well-trained therapists, aides, and teachers. God chose the skills, talents, and experiences that we were given to support her best life in each season of her life. No one can do much more than give her the unconditional love and endless patience that surrounds her, coupled with thirty hours of therapy a week to teach her communication, self-care, self-calming, task completion, and so much more.

Could I do better and more than I do now for Abigayle? Yes, if I did not also have a job (which supports Abigayle's therapy and medical care), husband, another daughter, dog, house to manage, bills to pay, and life's other general demands. Yes, I could do better if I got to "go home" as others do ... a home away from the increased demands. But wait ... this is my home 24/7 for 365 days of the year ... the home with increased demands for the last 16 years, every day and every night. Yes, in a perfect world where I could pause tantrums by snapping my fingers. Yes, in a perceived perfect world with lots of support, time, breaks, sleep, and vacation time. Yes, in a perfect world, everyone does better.

Fortunately, the pressure is off ... because we do not live in a perfect world. We live in a world where doing our best is good enough—for me, anyway! I have never pretended to be the best at providing therapy for Abigayle, as that is not a gift of mine. However, God gave me access to incredible therapists who are doing an amazing job. Most importantly, God gave *me* Abigayle, and He provides exactly what I need to be the best mom according to His perfect plan.

When people say they could do better, I say "Bring it on!" Yet, I've never had someone to seriously take on the challenge—only those who like to judge on the sidelines of my life. No one has asked to walk in my shoes for a day, week, or even a few hours. It's far too easy to judge from the sidelines, and it never feels good to be the recipient of the judgment. No one is perfect! What is important to remember is that words matter, love matters, support matters, and we all matter according to our well-designed purpose(s) in life.

So, instead of judging, I am going to give people credit for how they are managing based on what burdens are before them and the unique gifts given to them. I will give them credit for the struggles in their lives that I can't see from the sidelines. I am going to feel for them during their times of struggle, not judge them or think of how I could manage a situation better with my own skills. I will continue to take the energy and moments I have to think of how I can help support others, rather than judging them from the sidelines.

*"It's easy to judge. It's more difficult to understand.
Understanding requires compassion, patience,
and a willingness to believe that good hearts
sometimes choose poor methods. Through judging,
we separate. Through understanding, we grow."*
Doe Zantamata

People have asked how George and I became so compassionate. The answer is by living life ... really living and experiencing life—for ourselves, and by peeking through the stained-glass window of the lives of those who have surrounded us or gone before us. We learned compassion by experiencing heartbreak, disappointment, loss, rejection, regret, shame, judgment, hopelessness, sadness, darkness, honest mistakes, hatred, and the general bitterness life can sometimes bring. We listened to our parents' lessons of love and generosity. Most importantly, George and I allowed our hearts to remain open despite life's attempts to harden us.

If I'm qualified and doing the right things for the right reasons when others judge me, I consider that to be their problem. How much of life are they missing out on by spending so much energy judging others? Life is too short, so don't waste it on what others may think of you. As I said, their judgment is based upon their own emptiness, cruelty, and self-doubt.

*"It is quite clear that between love and
understanding there is a very close link ... He who
loves understands, and he who understands loves.
One who feels understood feels loved, and one who
feels loved feels sure of being understood."*
Paul Tournier

daddy's girl

Now Put the Lesson to Work in Your Own Life ...

Lesson Learned:
Dismiss the judgment of others as ignorance

I have learned that the so-called "experts" don't always know the answers, and my answer may differ from that of others. Take a few minutes to realize your own strength and what you can draw upon within.

Who is your worst critic? Is it you?

- Sometimes we are our worst judge, which can both work for us and hinder us.
- Give yourself a little more credit today for making it through life—both the good times and the bad.
- Consider how your judgment of yourself affects those you love and others around you and how they relate to you and the rest of the world. Is it working for you or against you?
- If you are concerned about the judgment of others, ask yourself the following:
  - Do you respect the person and the judgment of those sharing their opinions?
  - Is there validity to their comment? If so, what do you need to address in your life to create changes in this area?
- Secure, loving people with the right things in mind don't spread negativity, so why are you listening to those who judge, who really don't have you in mind when they are speaking? They are only acting out of their own circumstances AGAINST you, not FOR you.
- No one knows you like you do. They cannot know what is best for you in a way that you can. Take advice, but filter it through what you know about yourself and your circumstances. Only you can make the right choice!

What are the words of others that have stayed lurking around, penetrating you at the deepest level and impacting you from day to day? Are the words you're dwelling on ones that you created?

- People often don't mean what they say. They say things because they are jealous, insecure, abused, limited thinkers, threatened, uneducated in areas, desperate, scared, and so much more.

What needs to be said that has been left unsaid? Remember, tomorrow is not promised to anyone, and words matter!

Reminder: Dismiss the judgment of others as ignorance

Life Lesson: Bad vibes emanate from bad people

Abigayle responds to the energy in her environment more than most. Since she does not have the ability to verbally express her feelings, she is typically physically reactive to them (i.e., tantrums, affection, and smiles). She has an amazing ability to see people for who they are on the inside.

Our family friend, Courtne, once told me that she wished she could bring Abigayle home with her and introduce her to certain people in her life just to see how Abigayle would respond to them. Abigayle has a keen ability identifying the good and bad in people. She sees the good—and the bad—in them almost instantly, and she trusts her instincts. She protects herself from others and gives extra attention and affection to the people who provide her comfort.

For Every Bad in Life There Is Also Good... Focus on the Good!

As I'm finishing my next-to-last edit of this book, an event occurred that I feel compelled to share. The feelings are still raw, as I just walked in the door and started to write to get it all out. As I've said, I'm not a crier. My family has rarely seen me cry (except during my Hallmark movies). Tonight, it was very different.

Tonight, I released a barrage of tears, crying so hard that you could hear my pain. I'm not sure why tonight was different versus the last 16 years of managing public tantrums—maybe it was a release of all of the emotions that came from reading and editing all the stories I've shared in this book. That could have left my emotions raw on the inside, more so than usual.

I also heard some music this week that I'd played for my father while holding his hand as he took his last few breaths last year, which brought out some emotions ... on top of dealing with tantrums for a few days, and a lack of sleep. This likely put me in a state of vulnerability that was unexpected and unusual for me. This experience reminded me of a life lesson included in this book: Life is imperfect and out of your control, so you might as well keep moving forward. We moved forward this day, but it will be remembered.

My husband very, very rarely leaves town. This weekend happened to include a special birthday of a friend's son, plus a work event that George would attend a few hours away. With George gone, it has been a trying few days with lots of hair-pulling. I'm not sure if it was Abigayle being on her cycle, her upset tummy, or the disruption in her schedule this week that put her over the edge a few times. George has been taking on a lot of Abigayle's care lately, since I have a new job. His absence alone is likely enough to cause a disruption in her behavior, but she also has been eating a new food, which could be what's affecting her tummy.

Since it's been quite a day, and it typically does not go well in stores when Abigayle is not feeling well, I delayed going to get her medicine until the right time today. Unfortunately, that time never came. She really needed the medicine, so we had to suck it up and make it happen. Outside, it was drizzling off and on, which did not help the situation. Sometimes rain can also be a trigger for Abigayle … or maybe it's something in the atmosphere when it rains.

We only had about 25 minutes left before the pharmacy closed, so we jumped in the car and hoped for the best. I did see the best in people tonight, but I also experienced a shocking level of selfishness that took its toll on me. As we pulled up, Abigayle let me know with her physical cues that she did not want to leave the car to go into the store. She reluctantly complied, though.

As we walked, a kind man approached us to see if we were okay, given the odd walking we were doing with her attached to me. She is as tall as I am now, so it's hard to hold her, and she sometimes wraps her legs around my ankles, forcing me to waddle walk like a sumo wrestler. This day, she was walking backwards while hugging and snuggling at my neck. I assured him that we were fine and thanked him for the offer of help.

Then, right as we were approaching the front door of the store, Abigayle spotted a fountain. She went over and plopped down on the wet ledge of the fountain in the rain. I have walked by that fountain without noticing it many times, so I did not think to park in a way to avoid walking by it to get to the store. Remember how I told you she loves water? If I'd remembered the fountain, I certainly would have gone out of my way to avoid it, knowing it would be a huge distraction and possibly trigger behaviors when I made her leave or did not let her climb into it. But as they say, "When in Rome."

So, I decided to let her have a second, and I sat down on the wet ledge beside her. I say "decided" but I know I didn't have much of a choice if I wanted to avoid her pulling me over to it or having a tantrum. Hoping for the best, we sat, and she put only her finger into the water. This is where relishing the moment comes in, as we enjoyed our time despite the rain and the clock ticking. As I was trying to get Abigayle up and into the store, I experienced another man walking up to ask if I needed help. This visit was turning into a journey!

We eventually made it into the store, wet pants and all ... but who cares, really? What mattered was that she went into the store. We really needed her medicine for her allergies and eczema, and to stay on schedule. As we waited in line for five minutes (which felt like five years), I talked to Abigayle, sang, hugged her, and we teeter-tottered back and forth to keep her engaged and waiting ... which is not one of her strong suits.

I knew it was asking a lot for her to wait, and I could tell by her behavior that she could set off at any moment. "Set off" could mean anything really—hair pulling, running off, plopping to the ground screaming, laying on the ground, and so much more. We've experienced them all in this store at one point or another. She may have smelled the unease and fear within me. Even still, we had to wait. There was one lady with some complications ahead of us and two people waiting in line behind us for about three of the five very long minutes.

Abigayle started trying to pull and push me away to walk off, so I kept trying unsuccessfully to redirect her. She is 16, so the struggle was quite noticeable, and a lady walked up to see if she could help ... and then another generous soul did the same. Finally, I started redirecting Abigayle and we walked back, having only been steps away with our pulling and pushing spectacle. As we were only five or so steps away, the lady who had been in front of us walked off with her prescription. I was in the midst of feeling a wave of relief that we would be able to get the prescription when the unexpected blew my mind ...

The lady who stood behind us for so long—and who saw the issues I was having with Abigayle—saw us coming back to the line for our turn. With a smile on her face, she quickly darted in front of us to beat us to the counter before we could take those final few steps. Tears started flowing from my eyes as I experienced her harsh selfishness. I was desperate for the medicine and saw no way at that point to get it. I did not have the luxury of waiting in line yet again, as Abigayle would certainly not allow it.

I wanted to ask the lady how she could jump ahead of us after seeing the struggles we'd had over the last few minutes, but Abigayle never got close enough for me to ask her quietly. I was in utter shock. Thoughts raced through my mind, as people were asking to help. I just did not know how to get help for what I needed safely and successfully. Knowing how hard it was to get Abigayle there and the struggles of waiting thus far, I knew there was no way that Abigayle would continue to wait for anything.

As I was managing Abigayle's physical behavior, people kept coming up to ask to help, and I was also trying to think of how to get the medicine all at the same time. I could not figure out what to ask for in that moment, as people were offering assistance. That was our only chance for the day at getting her medicine. The lady saw and heard our struggle but still darted to the counter. She did not walk—she *dashed* forward to beat us. How sad must her life be for her to behave so coldly and uncompassionately?

The story doesn't end there. Abigayle was directing me back outside, and I followed her this time, since I was not sure if the gentleman waiting behind the lady would let us ahead of him. When we go to other places and people see the struggle, they typically let us go ahead of them. Otherwise, the second pharmacy employee will jump from her activities to offer a quick and helping hand to get us through quicker. This was not the case on that night, and the differences made me appreciate those times even more.

Abigayle got outside, and I thought maybe, just maybe, I could give her some attention and then coerce her back inside. Remember, Abigayle cannot understand everything I say, so coercion is a bit different with her. Threats don't work, and she would not understand any bribe to get her to go back. So, as we walked out, we hugged, and then she started pulling my hair with both hands in different directions while pulling me to the ground. This was right in front of the store with many, many onlookers. We were both on the ground in the rain, so I pulled her close to sit on my lap and hugged her to get her to calm down.

As she was pulling my hair and pulling me to the ground, a gentleman asked if he could help. She would only lash out at him too if he intervened, so I thanked him and shared why she was struggling. I held her and rocked her as tears escaped me. I've dealt with her tantrums in public before, but I have not experienced many instances where people were not supportive and helpful. I was still in shock that the lady had not let us get our medicine and be on our way. I also cannot put much blame on Abigayle—as I've mentioned, she can smell weakness. I felt very weak in that moment.

As I sat there, another gentleman told me he would put my purse by me, since I'd just thrown it onto the ground to get Abigayle to stop pulling my hair. He was concerned the purse was getting rain in it, but that was not a care of mine in that moment. He offered to help and stood there a few steps away for many minutes, even though I declined his help. He asked, "What's her name?" I often hear that question from kind souls planning to pray for her. The gesture warmed my heart! Through my tears, I let him know she just needed a minute and would leave when she was ready. I kept pulling up to leave, but she pulled me back down to the ground. We sat there on the concrete in the dark, the sprinkling rain coating our shoulders, rocking back and forth. I gave into the moment, instead of fighting it.

Moments later, Abigayle stood up and smiled. Then she walked off happily—as if nothing had happened. She reset and was on her way back into the store, where we found the pharmacists talking behind their closed bars just three minutes after they closed. Nothing else we went there to get mattered in that moment. I just wanted to get home, but Abigayle had other plans when she saw the fountain again. I thought, *we may be here for hours.*

Abigayle is as tall as I am, but stronger. She's also very stubborn. She knows she can overpower me, so I only have so many ways to get her to do what is needed, including managing my tone and facial expressions for happier times. We sat on the wet ledge once again until

I thought I saw lightning. This time, I was successful in hurrying her along to the car to go "bye-bye" as I told her. She loves going bye-bye, but sometimes loves water more. God was definitely with us this night, as not much else would get Abigayle to leave the water after such a short time playing in it. She does not understand the danger from the weather, so I know I had help from above.

As I process the event, I will focus my thoughts on two things:

1. I honestly had so many kind people walk up to me in the few minutes we were there that I don't even remember how many there were, for which I am thankful.
2. I expect the event gave a lasting impression of compassion for those who witnessed it or offered to help. I will also pray for more compassion to be experienced in this world.

I'm not entirely sure why I cried tonight. Was it the shock from the lady's selfish behavior, my desperation and failure to get Abigayle's medicine, the generosity and compassion of those good Samaritans, or the fact that I was reading this book, which can bring out so many buried emotions from the past? Tonight, as I have processed the situation, I remember the lessons my mom taught me at an early age, and I conclude that this event will not be wasted. I will grow from it, seek to understand, and focus on the silver lining of it all.

As I shared this story with my sweet neighbor and friend, Beth, she told me to put her on speed dial! My other friends sitting around the table all nodded and offered the same. They also prompted me to move to mail order medications, which is a great idea. I must make time to figure it out! Again, I could focus on the one lady in the store who shocked my conscience, or on the great gifts of many angels offering me help. I chose the latter. What would you choose?

I choose to be grateful for anything and
everything beautiful I experience in my life.
Human kindness is at the top of the list!

Now Put the Lesson to Work in Your Own Life ...

Lesson Learned:
Bad vibes emanate from bad people

I have learned that bad people exist, though they are rare. Most are just acting out of their own scared and desperate insecurities. Take a few minutes to think about those you surround yourself with and those who surround themselves with you.

We are all smarter than we give ourselves credit for, and we know more than we give our attention. We can feel the vibes people emanate, but often we don't trust our instincts. For us, it may not be life or death, as it could be for a vulnerable child with autism. Still, it's critical to pay attention to the vibes people exude and to give your resulting feelings some merit. Trust yourself and that feeling. It always saves me from pain, heartache, or other losses down the road. It will pay off for you!

We all impact those around us through the energy we contribute to our environment. Stay aware of this dynamic and create positive energy in your interactions, but also protect yourself from those around you who will infuse negativity into your world.

With whom have you surrounded yourself, and whom are you serving?

- There is nothing like replacing negative energy with positive energy. I love doing nice things for people unexpectedly, even if it is just sending a thoughtful note. It does more for my energy than that of others.
- Bad actors can impact the best of your character if you allow their ugliness and negativity to continually penetrate your environment, ears, and soul.

Who brings out the best and the worst in you?

- Are you accepting "scraps" or bad vibes from anyone? For instance, are you accepting less than what you deserve in a relationship because you do not *think* that you deserve more, are scared of the consequences if you ask for more, or have diminished expectations since you have not previously experienced more from others?

- Why not put deliberate effort on multiplying the good by surrounding yourself with people who can naturally bring it out in you? Abigayle's smile or a hug from Natalie is all I need to reset on a bad day. Who is surrounding you that can offer the same?

- Limit your interactions with (and tolerance for) those who bring out the worst in you, if you cannot sever ties altogether. You need to multiply the best in you, not the worst. Make changes today and reap benefits immediately!

- If you decide to make wholesale changes in those who surround you, rely on your faith and relationship with God to see you through to the other side of your journey. Remember, you are never truly alone. He is always with you ... both in the good times and the more challenging of times. Lean on him for your strength to see it all through. Be patient and watch all that he will do for you and those he will bring to you. Once you commit to positive change, stay the course and watch miracles happen!

Reminder: Bad vibes emanate from bad people

Life Lesson: Saving myself is all up to me ... and God, of course!

While I can depend on God to always look over me, I also understand that I have a personal responsibility to do the work that He asks of me. I don't get a free pass in life. We are all tasked with work to do, including pushing through the tough times that mold and grow us beyond our comforts in life. I understand I need to be ready when God gives me my assignment, so there is work to do to prepare. In addition, I know I have choices and that those choices have consequences. Even inaction has consequences on my life, so I choose to take inspired action to save myself from all that can try to bring me down in a day.

"Lazy hands make for poverty, but
diligent hands bring wealth."
Proverbs 10:4 (NIV)

"Diligent hands will rule, but laziness
ends in forced labor."
Proverbs 12:24 (NIV)

No matter how hard my circumstances get, I know I must take personal responsibility for my life. I cannot depend on others to always be available and willing to step in and save me from crises. It would be so nice, but I cannot even fully depend on having help on any given day or when I am desperate for help. No one can fully depend on anyone else, so I am thankful when help comes my way. I can truly only depend on grace from God!

Natalie sometimes tells me that other parents are more involved in reviewing their kid's homework and directing their decisions. In response, I let her know that my job is to make her strong and independent, so she can thrive when she is on her own. I told her that if she has a problem with my approach, she should talk to my mom, her Gran. She taught me to be a strong and independent woman.

Being dependent on others can be nice when I can rely upon it, but sometimes it comes at a great cost. Truly, the only saving that matters and is dependable is God's to give. It is impossible to depend on anything else, as I cannot control whether others will be available and willing to save me. God's love and support is endless and always available to ALL of us!

> *"But you will not leave in haste or go in*
> *flight; for the Lord will go before you, the*
> *God of Israel will be your rear guard."*
> Isaiah 52:12 (NIV)

While I would love to have someone rush in and save me during my moments of despair—and I'm sure Abigayle would likely love to be saved from her moments where she lacks self-control—no one can save us but ourselves. We must allow ourselves to be guided by God and take inspired action to save ourselves. On days I feel weak and I cannot do anymore, the only thing or person that can drag me out of my slump is myself. When I say myself, I mean with God's helping hand and strength to carry me through, as I know I am never alone in the struggle.

When I get frustrated and want to give up or yell out that I cannot take any more, I know my life needs centering. When I am off, others around me can become off too. As I have mentioned, Abigayle can smell weakness. She can be even more challenging during my toughest of times. On the more challenging of days, I must remember that I can only count on myself to get through it happily and without too many wasted moments. I, alone, have the ability to choose how I will react and can create a new perspective to change my circumstances—or, at least change their effect upon me. While I can impact the happiness of others, I cannot control anyone's happiness, but I can control my own. It doesn't always feel like I am controlling my happiness (or lack thereof) in the more challenging moments, but I know I am.

Not only do I get off-center, but sometimes I can also tell Abigayle is off-center by her frustrations and tantrums, even though she cannot verbalize it. I know that I cannot take Abigayle's challenges away from her, but I can give her love, acceptance, and my patience. I can show up as my best self, but that takes work. It is my responsibility to myself and Abigayle's responsibility to herself that we never let the circumstances of the day or those around us define how we experience our days. We must stay in control, and we can always bring a little light into the life of others through life-lifters: a smile, hug, gesture of love, some laughter, or a kiss.

When the little life-lifters don't work on the tougher of days, I know that means I need some extra time with my inner self to explore what I need at that moment in order to be the best version of myself. I know the challenging days are just a sign that I am not getting enough thinking time to center myself and reset my path. Sometimes this comes in the form of listening to music during golf cart rides, getting up early to spend time in nature (meaning the beach, for me), taking an extra-long shower, reading an inspiring book, watching my favorite Christmas Hallmark shows about successful women achieving their goals, spending time with my journal, or rewording my whiteboard with positive affirmations. Other times, I just need a little reminder of who I am at my core, what I can achieve, and what is important. I do what I can, but I also turn to God for guidance, support, grace, and love.

> *"Success is not final, failure is not fatal: it is*
> *the courage to continue that counts."*
> Winston Churchill

Now Put the Lesson to Work in Your Own Life ...

Lesson Learned:
Saving myself is all up to me ... and God, of course!

How do you determine when you are off-center in your life and in need of a reset?

- Are you self-aware and constantly looking at your circumstances to see if you are off-track with what you need and what is important?
- Consider taking time (weekly or monthly) to evaluate your life, where you want to go, and most importantly, why you have decided on this path.
- Sometimes people get fixated on what they think they *should* be doing instead of *why* they are doing it. Why do you want to be a writer, artist, doctor, dog groomer, manager, social worker, etc.? What are you really trying to get from that experience? Are you on the right path?

Is it time to reset? Do you feel you are experiencing your best life and being true to your authentic self within?

- Do you have plenty of energy?
- Do you feel drained?
- This is your first clue as to whether you are on the right path or need to reset.
- Are you focusing on your passions and bringing your talents into the world for others to experience?

We control so much in our lives beyond what we think about each day. We control a lot of who and what we surround ourselves with, which hugely impacts our experiences. Beyond ourselves, we need to look at what we have chosen to surround ourselves with and whether it serves or hinders our progress on our chosen path.

What is in your surroundings? Clutter? Do you have a tranquil environment of nice smells, views, and sounds? Do you have flowers and plants surrounding you? What can you do to make your experience of life more fulfilling and beautiful?

- Consider painting a room blue. There are studies on how certain colors can be uplifting.
- I love spraying eucalyptus and lemongrass scents in my shower. I also love the smell of orange or apricot shower gel and lotions.
- I sleep with an air purifier in my room. That way, I don't get disturbed with every little noise in the house, and I benefit from cleaner air!

With whom are you surrounding yourself and how are they serving you? How are you serving them?

- We can create a better life by looking around us to see who is influencing us and *being* influenced by us ... are we nurturing and serving others who are nurturing and serving us?
- It is so critical to have friends around you who inspire you to do and be better.
- Do you have friends keeping you stagnant or pushing you outside of your comfort zone?
- Do you have friends around you who are challenging you to think in new and innovative ways?
- Do you have friends around you who are stuck in the past and in a "this is how we do it" mode?
- Do you have friends lighting your way to a better future? Alternatively, are they darkening your path?

How are you spending your days? Are you fulfilled? Is it time for a change?

- After 10 years at my employer (in three different roles), I recently moved to a new company to go back into a field I'd enjoyed working in several years ago. I did this because I had a change of seasons in my life, and my old company and role no longer served me. Sometimes, our seasons in life change without us recognizing it. What about you?

When was the last time you spent quality time with yourself? When was the last time you spent alone time with God?

- It is up to you to tap into the resources available to you anywhere and at any time. The path will be made clear, your reprieve from the circumstances will come (either in the form of closure or a change of perspective), gifts will be given, or your answers will be evident.

One thing you can count on is that life will always go on, no matter how we are experiencing our days. We might as well decide to live out our moments sweetly by savoring the good in life, rather than ... well, you get the picture! We decide how our moments are to be lived and what will come of our future.

What have you decided for your future? You are the only one on this earth who knows exactly what you need and who you are deep inside. You are the only one who can spark your own light. Let's get started lighting that fire! We all must take personal responsibility for where we are today in order to know that we can make impactful changes for tomorrow.

What are you putting off or depending on others to do that is your responsibility to do?

Reminder: Saving myself is all up to me ... and God, of course!

Life Lesson: Self-preservation and boundaries are a must

Abigayle has her own targeted personal boundaries. Although she does not understand much of the world, she does know how to protect herself in *some* areas. For instance, she cannot be trusted at home around water sources or in the ocean, but she is very careful when playing in the pool. She somehow understands the danger of the pool and responds accordingly. She is fearless in the Gulf of Mexico, so we have to maintain several controls for her safety. She will also throw herself down in a tantrum and has other self-injurious behaviors, but sometimes with very controlled movements to protect herself physically.

her favorite place

she loves to play in the sand

Where she can identify possible danger, she has self-preserving mechanisms that kick into place; however, those same mechanisms will not keep her from running into the street. Thankfully, she has not been in a situation to understand the consequences of running in front of a car, but that means she doesn't see the need for such self-preservation. We can all learn from this differentiation.

When we know that we are walking towards danger by making poor decisions, it would be great for our self-preservation mechanisms to take control. Unfortunately, we tend to ignore the alarms and run towards danger instead. We do this for many reasons, including peer pressure and the desire for a quick fix. Some paths are within our control, and warnings should be heeded.

Abigayle does not answer to others the way I do. She never appears ashamed and does not apologize for making sure her needs are met and her boundaries respected. She just enforces the boundaries. Do you need to enforce boundaries to protect the life you have imagined for yourself? Sometimes it's hard to enforce boundaries in certain areas of our lives, but we are all worth the effort.

> *"Close some doors today. Not because of pride, incapacity or arrogance, but simply because they lead you nowhere."*
> Paulo Coelho

Beware of Good Intentions

Well-intentioned people and efforts are great, until they are not. When I found out I was pregnant with twins, people with good intentions gave me books on having twins and all the ways to excel in parenting them, including sleep schedules and what to expect from the pregnancy and early years. I displayed my own great intentions by reading the books to learn and figure out all the wonderful tips from those who had conquered birthing and parenting twins before me.

Well, the good intentions ended up putting me in a tailspin of stress and worry, and I was left with feelings of inadequacy. I finally gave the books to my husband and asked him to get rid of them. Sometimes information is good, but not in this case. Even the audiobooks I currently listen to have impacted my mood and mindset while writing.

Later, when Abigayle was diagnosed with a very rare syndrome, I again had good intentions of learning more and researching it. This was a HUGE mistake! I spent two days bawling when I read the horrific details of death and the devastation caused by consequences of the syndrome. I'd never read about it again until today, which is a bit easier, but still very difficult even though I've advanced my ability to absorb this information greatly over the years.

There is also more information available now, which creates greater balance than in the earlier days of the internet. Again, I was just trying to be a great mom and get to know my child back then. The more extreme stories on the internet were not what we were facing, so they were scary.

When the autism diagnosis came along, I knew I should be very targeted in my reading and not get overwhelmed with all the different views and options. This required me to establish boundaries for what I was taking into my mind, including the many references to high divorce rates. Reading about autism was rewarding in some of the more positive books, but sometimes I can get overwhelmed with the differing, and often bullying, views on social media. So, yes, it is great to research and great for people to share information, but I have to put up boundaries as to what I let my mind see and dwell on.

Now Put the Lesson to Work in Your Own Life ...

Lesson Learned:
Self-preservation and boundaries are a must

I have learned that I am the best person to protect myself, but that requires daily discipline in both the little and big moments. Take a few minutes to consider where you need to make adjustments in your life today.

What do you need to do today to take better care of and preserve your mind, body, and soul? Act today, before time flies by and greater problems arise.

What are your roadblocks to acting and living out your desires? What can you do about them?

Are you surrounding yourself with people who might be keeping you down or holding you back? What adjustments need to be made in your relationship with them?

What boundaries do you need to put up for your own self-preservation?

**"Being challenged is inevitable,
being defeated is optional."**
Roger Crawford

Reminder: Self-preservation and boundaries are a must

CHAPTER 9

EVERYONE IMPACTS THEIR SURROUNDINGS

NO MATTER WHETHER Abigayle intends to have an impact on others' lives or not, she always does. That does not necessarily mean it's always a *positive* impact, but every encounter with others can have a great impact. Judgment by limited thinkers may interfere with her being able to positively impact all who encounter her, but that is not her concern.

Her life is meant for a larger purpose than herself (as is true with all of us), and I am here to serve by caring for her while she creates more understanding, love, and compassion in the world. I've grown so much by serving her over the years, and I've watched her teach the masses through no words at all. I enjoy being on the sidelines and watching her bring a light out in others. It is truly an incredible experience to see how her mere presence can soften the hardest of hearts.

Life Lesson: The Ability to Share and Learn is a Gift No One Should Take for Granted

After years of just surviving the days, the realization of my life's purposes started to grow within me. I knew I had been blessed with the opportunity to serve Abigayle and share her amazingness with the world, but I also knew there was more. God gave me a strong nudge to write a book. While it seemed logical to write this exact book, I resisted. In fact, I wrote other books before this one and kept steering myself away by starting even more books.

I did not feel I had struggled in a way to validate the words I was writing, even though the truth in the stories tell a different story. Now that I have pushed through the hurdles, I am proud of what I can share—not just on my behalf, but on Abigayle's. I like to think she would type up something similar if she had the skills to do so! God has given me the resources and placed the desire in my heart, so now I am sharing my deeply personal stories with the world—which I can tell you is not very easy. I do it anyway, because I know it's what I am supposed to do whether I like it or not.

Time to Share, Teach, and Learn

My dad taught me to learn the value of others through their story and the lessons they share. There was not a day that went by or a place that my dad walked into where he did not get to know someone's life story. We all have our tragedies and triumphs to share with the world through our words, but few take the time to share and listen.

These days, I see less and less listening and more deaf ears diminishing the value of others among us. This is a tragedy, along with those who ignore the value in learning from each other's history and perspectives. It is sad to find so many people in the world shutting off the ability to learn from others by turning a deaf ear.

There is always more to learn from those who surround us or have gone before, so we do not repeat the same mistakes. We do not only learn from the messages and the people we agree with and who agree with us—we can also learn from those we don't agree with, and they can learn from us. Without keeping an open mind and open ear, we risk making the same mistakes or taking for granted what we have accomplished over time.

I now see how I am a better person for having encountered every single person in my life, no matter the positivity or negativity of the encounter. I try to always look for the good in someone, rather than focus on "what is not" within them. We are all evolving at our own pace and with unique resources, and I know that all encounters with others support my growth in one way or another. I consider how God puts experiences and people into my path according to their purpose to teach compassion and my need for growth, so all experiences cannot be perfect all the time.

I look inward to see my contribution in the relationship, rather than always looking to the other person to make things right among us. For instance, with Abigayle, I consider how my mood for the day might be impacting hers, which could be a trigger for a tantrum. Lately, I think people are getting too singularly focused on what they know to be right, rather than considering where there can be more than one acceptable view of any situation or experience.

Love, Understanding and Grace

I don't always know what Abigayle understands or doesn't understand— since she cannot talk or otherwise confirm her understanding with communication techniques in all cases. Also, she does not have any way to ask for help—beyond her tantrums or guiding us to a general area—and she's unable to say exactly what she needs. We all know she is super intelligent in some ways and has amazing coping skills, for which I am very grateful, but that is not always enough.

Tonight, I told her to turn off the light, but she closed the door. I told her again, and she opened the door. She looked a bit unsure of what to do and even looked at the light switch as an option. She knew I needed something in that general area by looking at me, but she was not exactly sure what. So, she decided to close the door again. She kept looking at me for confirmation that closing or opening the door solved my request. Abigayle had the best intentions, but she could not figure it out no matter how hard she tried or how many times I spoke to her.

We give Abigayle a lot of credit for being tricky and smart, but everything still does not click for her every time. I think many of us are the same! We can all use a little help here and there to make the right decisions based upon what we are being told within, by God! We may have some general sense of what he is telling us or nudging us to do, but God also puts people in our pathway to support us on our journey (or provide support for another on theirs).

> **"Whoever loves discipline loves knowledge,**
> **but whoever hates correction is stupid."**
> Proverbs 12:1 (NIV)

Sometimes, we need a little help from each other to better understand which actions we need to take. So, next time you see someone not acting in a way that you feel is right or acceptable, ask yourself if there is something for you to learn from them. If not, consider what you can do to help them find their right way—not *your* right path, but theirs. You are in their path for a reason, so try to figure out what that is and take inspired action. For me, I am here to serve Abigayle so she can impact all who encounter her. Part of that is writing this book and passing along all the lessons I've learned to you, dear reader.

As my last lesson, I thought it would be fitting to focus on how sharing ourselves and our resources can benefit society. As mentioned in several places throughout this book, the world is hurting, people are hurting, and "We, the People" are the only ones who can save us! Each of us has a part to play in the resurrection of lending a helping hand or promoting goodness, love, kindness, compassion, generosity, forgiveness, and all other things good in our humanity. Yes, we are just one, but Abigayle is just one and her impact is mighty, without words!

"Be devoted to one another in love. Honor
one another above yourselves."
Romans 12:10 (NIV)

"Do not be overcome by evil, but overcome evil with good."
Romans 12:21 (NIV)

Now Put the Lesson to Work in Your Own Life ...

Lesson Learned:
The ability to share and learn is a gift no
one should take for granted

This lesson is one of the most important of all. No one person on this earth can encompass all—only God is all-knowing. God placed many of his children on this earth to serve a broader purpose collectively, not individually. We all have a part to play.

We all have something to share. No group is more important than another, even if you disagree with them holistically. We all *exist* according to our purpose, but we still must ask ourselves if we are actually *serving* according to our purpose, or if we're serving selfishly.

> *"We have different gifts, according to the grace given to each of us. If your gift is prophesying, then prophesy in accordance with your faith; if it is serving, then serve; if it is teaching, then teach; if it is to encourage, then give encouragement; if it is giving, then give generously; if it is to lead, do it diligently; if it is to show mercy, do it cheerfully."*
> Romans 12:6-8 (NIV)

Now, I ask you ...

- Do you have a role model or someone you strive to be more like? What is it about them that influences you? Why is this important to you? What are you doing to grow from your experience of them?
- What is the role you have been playing in the lives of those around you? Has it been one that promotes and is considered positive or is it diminishing the value of another?
- Have you considered the impact you are having on others around you by both what you are doing and what you know <u>you need to do</u>, but which you may be avoiding?

- What can you learn from those around you?
  - What *should* you learn from others around you?
- How are you serving others today?
  - How *should* you be serving?

I pray for more kindness and grace
being offered to all in this world.
We could *all* use it!

Reminder: The Ability to Share and Learn is a Gift No One Should Take for Granted

CHAPTER 10
TAKEAWAYS

S INCE YOU ARE worth the effort, what lessons will you take away?
I hope you were able to take away a few key thoughts from the
lessons shared, and that they will positively impact your life. I often
tell people that I would be so empty and spoiled if autism had not
come into my life. I cannot imagine my life without it. I often hear
my dad's voice in my ear telling me that Abigayle is here on earth to
teach us all. The lessons she teaches us are plentiful, and they keep
coming. Every day is an opportunity for me to see the bright side of
autism and other developmental differences.

> *What opportunities are you being given today*
> *that enable you to look at your more troubling*
> *circumstances in a brighter and more positive light?*

> *Are you a product of your surroundings*
> *or of deliberate intentions?*

> *Is it time to remember the old you and get back the*
> *best parts of who you are deep inside ... that person*
> *of the past that you have not seen in a while ... the*
> *strong, the dreamer, the doer of the impossible?*

> *Our days are numbered, so why not start making the most*
> *of your days and increasing the precious moments again?*

You have spent the time reading all the lessons I've learned from
parenting Abigayle *through no words at all*. Do any of them resonate
as a priority for you? If so, pick three (or more) of the lessons you
wish to prioritize, and take intentional action on them today. Decide

what these chosen lessons mean for your life and what you can do to incorporate them today.

Take deliberate actions for change and don't waiver when the going gets tough. Abigayle is living proof that it is possible to get more out of our moments, no matter our circumstances. After you have made lasting progress in one of your chosen priorities, pick another lesson.

Now, it's time to pay it forward. If this book has spoken to you regarding another person you know who needs one or more of these messages, consider either sharing the book with them or making a deliberate effort to share the message(s). We all have a responsibility to support more kindness and love in this world, so share the messages and encourage others to do the same.

We cannot afford to spend our energy complaining or worrying, as that same energy can be used to create more goodness in the world. We should all create a wave of compassion and love that will multiply. What can you do to help another advance in life or get out of a rut or hole? Do it!!!

> *"Remember this: Whoever sows sparingly*
> *will also reap sparingly, and whoever sows*
> *generously will also reap generously."*
> 2 Corinthians 9:6 (NIV)

I have encountered many wonderful acts of human kindness and love through my opportunity of parenting Abigayle and Natalie. They continue to teach me, touch others, and inspire greatness wherever they go. As I've said, no one can have a bad day when they look at the bright smile on Abigayle's face or get a warm hug from a loved one—in my case, Natalie. We all can give in more ways than we are today, so think about new ways to bring more joy to others. A genuine smile or an unexpected "I love you" spoken to another can make all the difference in their world, and it does not cost a thing. Collectively, we can *gain* more purpose in our lives by helping ignite others to *give* more and *get* more out of their moments, which will add up to a great life!

"Have I not commanded you? Be strong and courageous.
Do not be afraid; do not be discouraged, for the
LORD your God will be with you wherever you go."
Joshua 1:9 (NIV)

Abigayle works through the barrier of being non-verbal to teach in her own unique way. Many times, the lessons and inspiration come at a great price. I respect all parents, caretakers, and the children diagnosed with autism for what they endure along their life's journey. I continue to have faith that there is a silver lining of goodness that can be found in the struggle.

"And we know that for those who love God all
things work together for good, for those who
are called according to his purpose."
Romans 8:28 (ESV)

CHAPTER 11
WHO HAS WHAT IT TAKES?

"Mothers of children with autism have stress levels comparable to combat veterans."
University of Wisconsin-Madison

FOR MANY PARENTS with a child who has been diagnosed with a disability, including autism, most days have the impact that one might experience in the early days and years of caring for a newborn or young child. That same level of care must be sustained throughout their life, even by aging parents. Parenting a child with one disability can be tough, but many times, children have multiple disabilities to manage.

Although our Abigayle has been diagnosed with multiple disabilities, autism has had the most impact on our family and is always our main focus. Doctors have told us that they can treat Abigayle as they would other children diagnosed with autism, but we cannot expect the same results. It is always a mystery for us as to how she will respond to treatments. She is complicated, and it is a journey, as autism affects each person in a unique way. We just have to go with whatever her journey brings to us.

"Trust in the LORD with all your heart and lean not on your own understanding; In all your ways acknowledge Him, and He shall direct your paths."
Proverbs 3:5-6 (NKJV)

There are many ways to view the silver lining of our experiences. As for my silver linings, I can tell you that I have learned so much about myself while parenting sweet, precious Abigayle through some very challenging times. Before Abigayle came into my world, I remember watching a child diagnosed with autism on the news. The thought hit me, "I don't think I could be a mother to a child with autism." I did not think I had what it takes, but little did I know. So, what does it take?

Courage!

We all have more courage than we know. Sometimes our courage is revealed in opportunities of heroism that come about in a flash, while other times we are heroic in just showing up for the challenges day in and day out. Sometimes we choose to display our heroism, and sometimes the responsibility is thrust upon us ... a do-or-die situation.

One Thanksgiving a few years ago, I decided that I should finally join some parent groups so I could share stories, learn from others, and otherwise know what is going on in the autism community. Sadly, this journey led to days and days of tears pouring out of me. The desperation of some moms and the inability to help every one of them was more than I could handle. I wish I could say that I found support in these forums, but I only saw bickering and fighting as to what therapy is appropriate, as well as judgment of poor parents who found themselves in very difficult and dangerous situations having to make tough choices. Eventually, I had to cut ties with multiple forums.

This experience made me think hard about why autism exists and what it takes to be a mom with a child who has been diagnosed with autism (or for some, more than one child diagnosed). I also considered what it takes to live with autism. So many moms shared that they could not do it anymore, but they did. After much thought, I determined it takes ...

Courage!

Last year I went through a very difficult time trying to get therapy services for Abigayle approved by my insurance company, a challenge that is still ongoing. It was a grueling process for my family, the therapist, the therapy facility, my company's human resources department, and the insurance employees. It took many months and many, many papers and conversations to get her the therapy that has been so critical to her recent successes in life. The therapy gave her confidence that she can do what she sets her mind to do. We have seen so many critical improvements to her enjoyment in life, like an increased ability to redirect from her tantrums, plus reduced tantrums overall.

During one of the calls with my insurance company, the case manager told me that she does not know how I do it, and if she were me, she would crawl into bed in a fetal position under the covers and just stay there. Of course, this is not an option when you have a household to care for, including a child who gets into everything and can make anything dangerous. So, how did I manage through that extremely challenging time with Abigayle home full-time and all the stresses related to her not getting critical therapy that she needs?

Again, Courage!!!

As I consider the courage it takes for me to get through the challenging times in life and in my world with autism, I consider how Abigayle is the one who has to get up every single day in a world that is beyond any control for her. She has so much working against her, more than just autism, but she's always full of courage. She deserves so much for all that she endures! I am glad that I am the person chosen to give back to Abigayle. What does it take for Abigayle to prevail day after day?

Courage!

When I think of courage, I think about ...

- o Grandparents with custody of their grandchildren diagnosed with autism, and sometimes their own children too. I think of how their bones and energy are not as strong as mine, but they take on the challenges.
- o Single parents—as the divorce rate is much higher for families with autism—who take on this life without a break or a strong shoulder during the tougher times.

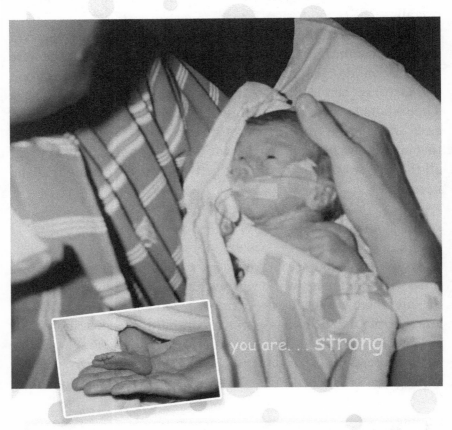

you are... strong

"While we are sad for you to have any challenges,
we know you will succeed...
Life will be harder for you than others,
but you are so very strong."

(Letter from Mom to Abigayle on the day of autism diagnosis)

- ○ New parents who have entered this unknown world by adopting an autistic child. (Some of these parents may not discover the diagnosis for a few more years.)
- ○ Siblings in the household, who manage the best they can under a different kind of life—one filled with tantrums, less attention, and the pressure of taking on responsibilities after the death of the parents.
- ○ The desperate parents who don't know how they can hold on and take another day.
- ○ Caretakers who share their time and love.
- ○ The children with autism who are working hard to fit into a mold of what the expectations are for them.

Yes, courage is required for all of us to get through the tough times in life, and we all have those times! I find my courage through my faith. It is what keeps me positive and gets me out of bed to face another day.

I have a dream that all parents with children diagnosed with autism can find a place of worship and support. It is not easy to find a place of worship that families can attend together... or at least it has not been for me. Sometimes, the courage is available within the strength of many, not just the individual. This is why it's so important to find a pathway to worship for families with a diagnosis of autism. I am thankful for many electronic forums to engage and worship, but there is nothing like having a church community around you, supporting you and your family in person.

> *"No one will be able to stand against you all the days of your life. As I was with Moses, so I will be with you; I will never leave you nor forsake you."*
> Joshua 1:5 (NIV)

CHAPTER 12

THE BRIGHT SIDE: THE TENDER JOYS I HAVE EXPERIENCED THROUGH THE LOVE AND KINDNESS OF OTHERS

T HERE ARE SO many wonderful moments, beyond what I can share here, when I have been touched by others in my journey with Abigayle. I feel the world could use some good stories to counter all the conflict and craziness we are all experiencing in the world today, so I am sharing some of our touching moments below. My family has been so fortunate to have wonderful, loving and compassionate people surrounding us. We've also had those who've appeared in support of us at just the right time.

> *"Blessed are they who see beautiful things in humble places where other people see nothing."*
> Camille Pissarro

Never Underestimate a Play Date

When the twins were in kindergarten, I once asked a mom of a child with developmental differences if her daughter could come over for a play date with my girls. This little girl did not have autism, but she did have some struggles similar to Abigayle's. The mom cried and said that was the first invitation her daughter had ever received for a play date.

Concerned, she started explaining all the different things I would have to be prepared to manage. I assured her that they were not dissimilar to what I was already managing with Abigayle. This experience touched me and taught me that you never know the impact you can have on others for the simplest things. I considered it natural to ask for a play date, but it meant the world to this mom and to other moms I have shared with similarly.

Neighborhood Love

Currently, Abigayle is famous in our neighborhood. I swear everyone knows her name—even strangers. Many have approached me while I'm with Abigayle to ask if they can bring their dog over as an opportunity for Abigayle to connect. Others have shared that they pray for Abigayle, and our neighbor Ron even offered me a backup golf cart to use if ours ever breaks down. Matt and Valerie recently let us borrow their golf cart during her school break while our golf cart was getting new tires. This really saved us a lot of tantrums.

Outside, everyone in our neighborhood waves at her and calls out her name. Our close friends, Steve and Deb, always greet Abigayle with the biggest smiles and a high five. Oh, and how Abigayle loves driving by Jan's house to hear her yell out and wave. Just last week, our neighbor John stopped his car to tell Abigayle how beautiful she is and tell me how lucky I am.

There is always a showering of love for Abigayle as we navigate the neighborhood. It was not surprising when Deb shared that she has been asked if she knows Abigayle when she introduces herself to strangers and shares that she lives in our neighborhood. During the last edit of this book, the local neighborhood magazine *Inside the Gates* asked to interview us and take pictures of Abigayle to feature her on the cover. She's famous!

Sometimes I feel as if we are driving through an "Abigayle Parade"—waving and saying hi to her many fans. I have been stopped in the middle of the road many, many times while handling a tantrum, and strangers often stop to help. Abigayle has been famous in most of the neighborhoods where we have lived, including our temporary housing. At the pool, Abigayle was known for running up to other people to join them or see what they were doing, eating, or drinking. The stories of our many wonderful neighbors and their acts of kindness could fill an entire book. We are blessed!

Teresa, a lady in our neighborhood, saw Abigayle having some struggles and asked if she could give her something to help her through hard times. It was a shell with "Philippians 4:13" written on it. Philippians 4:13 (NKJV) states, "I can do all things through Christ who strengthens me." I was very touched by her thoughtfulness, especially as that verse is a go-to for me when I need strength or some relief. The true kindness and loving gestures of these people are incredible phenomenon for me. These experiences make me feel less alone, and they remind me of my many blessings.

Sand Traps Look FUN!!!

In August of 2020, Abigayle and I experienced a moment of disappointment along with a moment of kindness. I saw a beautiful sunset and sped over in my slow golf cart to the other side of our neighborhood to catch it at 7:30 p.m., which is a little late for Abigayle. Abigayle and I parked by other golf carts to get a picture of her with the incredibly beautiful sunset in the background. Unfortunately, Abigayle had other plans. She bolted towards the sand trap (sidenote: I called it a sandbox, but my husband corrected me) on the golf course shortly after I parked. I ran after her, begging her to stop running and to instead go "bye-bye" with me. She laid on the ground while I pulled at her arms and clothes to get her up, trying to keep her out of the sand trap inches away. She was sliding on her back to get into it, and she was winning the battle.

I was trying so hard, and she started ripping at my shirt and pulling my hair out of its ponytail and off my scalp. I was really struggling—to stay standing, keep her out of the sand trap, get her to stop pulling my hair, *and* keep her from tearing off my shirt completely. It was a bit scary for a few moments, as much of my skin under my shirt was already showing as she pulled on my shirt from the ground. I was trying to keep my clothes on and my dignity!

All the while, a woman was screaming at us *repeatedly*, "Girls, move … move … girls move … we are trying to play golf!!!" It was clear that she was somehow oblivious as to what was happening, despite the very odd and unexplained behaviors. I yelled back, "She's autistic, and I am TRYING!!!" I did not have a clue that in the midst of the other golf carts, which were a bit off to the side, there were still people playing golf in the same area. Abigayle had run off so fast, and there were so many people, I could not have known. When we pulled into this area next to the water on the golf course, there were about 20 other people on golf carts viewing the sunset. It was clear we were not just hanging out during the tussle, but the lady was not pleased with the interruption.

As for the moment of kindness ... two nice men walked up and calmly asked if it would help for them to bring our golf cart close to us, as Abigayle was by that point hanging onto me like a toddler (though she's almost my size), with her legs wrapped around only one of mine. It was quite a walk, with her full 100-pound body hanging on my one side. The two men were so kind in driving the golf cart over, but Abigayle still had my hair in her hands and was still trying to pull me to the ground. They asked if they could further help, and they picked up the hat Abigayle threw to the ground. I did get a picture *without any smiles*, but I thought to myself that I certainly won't try that again! Later, I tried it again with the support by our dear friends Steve and Debbie ("Deb") Depew. We ended up with many beautiful pictures of Abigayle, which is such a blessing.

Friendships are Invaluable

George and I also have some dear friends from Birmingham, Alabama, who visit here and there. Ian, George's best friend, is fearless when it comes to helping. He'll assist with our golf cart rides for Abigayle or will pitch in on other small, but extremely helpful, family responsibilities—like taking our dog for a walk. He is a tremendous help when he visits, as Abigayle's demands for care never stop and are like those of a toddler. This means we cannot just run to the store and leave her at home alone, even at 16 years of age.

Abigayle

Natural
Beauty

Picture Credit:
Deb DePew (Sunsetcelebrations@yahoo.com)

Ian is so gentle with Abigayle. He talks to her like he would any teenager. He understands that there is a lot to do to keep things running in the household while also giving her 24/7 attention and care, so he is not demanding of his own needs when in town. The extra support is always welcomed, as there is always more to do than we get done in our household. My mom says it takes a village to provide Abigayle the proper time, care, and attention. She is loved!

While some are fearful of caring for Abigayle for valid reasons, Ian and his family have been with us through our entire journey with the girls. They have been a treasure for our family, even taking a few turns driving Abigayle around the neighborhood. I also have a friend, Lisa, who is happy to pitch in when she is in town. Our friends are great blessings to us!

Ian recently reminded me of a time he was driving Abigayle around on the golf cart. She was playing with her favorite stuffed animal, when suddenly it fell out of the golf cart at a busy intersection. He had to keep going because there were cars coming from all directions toward the spot where it fell. He was hoping that she would not start to fuss, because he knew she loved this particular stuffed animal.

Ian had a huge dilemma: no matter what he did, a meltdown was likely imminent. Whether he stopped the golf cart or left the doll, either action would likely cause a meltdown for Abigayle. No matter the cause, a meltdown in a crowded street is not easy to manage safely.

Ian knows very well that Abigayle does not have any patience when the golf cart stops. When I stop, she will take her hand and put it on my foot, directing it towards the gas pedal. She will do this repeatedly or just meltdown as a form of rebellion when I don't comply. Some days I can get a few more seconds than others. Ian did not know what to do, because he could not leave her in the golf cart to go pick it up only steps away from the street without risking her running off or melting down.

There were just too many cars to trust the situation would be safe long enough for him to recover the stuffed animal. Just as his mind was getting discombobulated with the options, he was shocked to see people stopping the traffic to get the doll and bring it to her. Seeing strangers go out of their way to make sure her doll was returned really made an impression on him that will last a lifetime.

Always up to **something!**

Picture Credit:
Lauren Deman

It is not easy for people to pitch in with Abigayle, even if they have the desire. George and I know what Abigayle is capable of and are trained to stay on constant watch. Many sitters have been told of the dangers, but people still underestimate her. We must consider not only Abigayle's safety, but also the safety of others with good intentions. Once we had a friend take Abigayle for a golf cart ride, and the situation ended with multiple security units trying to help figure out how to get her settled and back on the golf cart to get her home.

Moms are Golden

No one has contributed more to our family than my mom. While in her 60s, and now in her 70s, her support has been critical and invaluable to our family's survival. She helped me work through some of the most severe times and still works to help me identify the differences between Abigayle's autism and just plain bad behavior! Natalie has always been so precious, rarely displaying bad behavior, so it is great to have Mom with her broader experience to know the differences. She and Abigayle have had a few "battles of the will," and my mom has always prevailed.

My mom was so wonderful when Natalie was brought home from NICU while Abigayle was still there. We had to spend a lot of time at the hospital, but I did not want to expose Natalie to the hospital as a premature baby herself. Mom would take Natalie home with her for periods of time to allow Abigayle and Natalie to both have the attention they needed in two separate places. As a new mom, this was invaluable to me.

The most critical turning point was when Mom solved the problem of our sleepless nights. Abigayle always fought bedtime, so I would rock her to sleep. This was a problem when she would awaken in the night because rocking her was the only way to get her back to sleep. When she would wake up, she would start screaming, so I would run in and rock her to sleep again to keep her from waking the entire household. This led to many sleepless nights for me.

My mom came in and helped shift Abigayle into a new routine in which she could comfort herself to sleep without any rocking. I was always so tired, and many times overwhelmed, so sometimes the simplest solutions were too much for me. My mom helps me fill in the holes, as I have a demanding job on top of caring for the family. Time and time again, Mom has worked her magic.

How Terese Serves

My family has also been enormously blessed by a kind friend, Terese, who we met when Abigayle turned six. Terese has watched Abigayle for us many times, including two times that allowed us to go on vacations. If not for her and my mom occasionally stepping in, George and I could not take time away together overnight. We met Terese while living in California, and she now visits us once a year in Florida.

In 2020, during COVID-19, knowing we did not have any of our usual help, Terese stayed with us for over a month and really saved our lives. She takes the challenges in stride and continues to come back to enjoy time with Abigayle and the rest of the family. She does this out of pure love, selflessness, and generosity.

There are so many kind people in this world, and Abigayle tends to reveal them. I have been told more than once that her smile is infectious. Abigayle has changed the lives of many when they have seen her strength and experienced her love.

The Pure Acts of Kindness by Strangers

> **"People are not disturbed by things, but
> by the views they take of them."**
> Epictetus

Countless times, a tantrum in public has caused spilled food, drinks, and more. I have experienced impressive and disappointing reactions to Abigayle in public. Three stories come to mind most vividly when thinking of complete strangers who have shown generosity and kindness to our family.

Once, in a Publix, Abigayle was triggered and instantly threw her new drink, which I had just opened, fanlike across the floor. She then began running and screaming through the grocery store. I thought giving her the drink would keep her busy and her hands satisfied, but she had other ideas. George and I are continually presented with the need to make split-second decisions. Of course, I had to sprint after her myself through a crowd of people passing eight grocery isles before I finally caught her. Catching her was only the first step. Then, somehow, I had to find a way to get her to play along with the rest of our grocery store trip.

It is so hard for me to leave a massive mess for others to clean up, but in these moments, I have to give in and let it go. All the while, Abigayle was laughing loudly, almost uncontrollably. Although I caught her, I certainly could not contain her enough to clean up the mess. The people there told me not to worry and that they would handle it all. They responded with a smile and without shooting daggers of anger at me. Trust me, I have received many looks in grocery stores from customers frustrated by my child throwing a tantrum or exhibiting odd behavior, so I am thankful for the grace I received that day.

Another time, while at CVS, Abigayle had a tantrum in which she threw herself into a stand of many, many Kinder Joy eggs—all while kicking, screaming, and pulling me down to the ground by my hair. What looked like 100 eggs flew all over the floor in every direction. As I calmed and redirected Abigayle and went to pay for my things, the cashier told me, with a smile, not to worry about the mess and to have a good day. This was such a touching experience for me, as I know we had left her a lot to clean up, and I was helpless to give her a hand.

I dreaded going into the store with Abigayle that day because she seemed a little agitated. With the Kinder Joy tantrum, my fears were realized, but the experience gave me a wonderful opportunity to witness human kindness, which I can carry with me forever. I am also thankful I could contain Abigayle long enough to pay and then take my purchases home. Many times, we've had to leave stores without a thing.

Lastly, a sweet lady, Shantika, at our local Chick-fil-A drive-through never misses an opportunity to engage with Abigayle. If she sees her through the window, she will run across the room just to say hi with her huge, infectious smile. She always pays attention to Abigayle's order too, because she knows what Abigayle likes. She always inquires when I don't get Abigayle her favorite drink. I typically respond by sharing that Abigayle has been throwing her drinks in the car that week, so I cannot chance it.

These individuals have true, generous spirits that warm my soul. There are countless other stories too. We even had a physician give Abigayle an examination in our car when she refused to stop screaming as she was laying on the floor of his office. I expected that we would leave without being seen, but he was creative. As you can imagine, catheters and blood draws on previous visits made her scared to death of a doctor's office. No one was going to get her to go into the examination room. I have even experienced a generous neurologist's hug at the end of our appointment, as she knows the toll Abigayle's challenges can take on our family.

> *"Everyone you meet is fighting a battle you*
> *know nothing about. Be kind. Always."*
> Brad Meltzer

There are so many good people out there doing good things and being generous, which can greatly impact the life of another. We all must take the time and effort to look up from our devices and truly experience these world changers. During the stressful moments I just described, I could have easily focused on the embarrassment of Abigayle's tantrums and what it was doing to ME instead of thinking of the generous gestures of others. I am grateful that I did not just pass through those experiences without recognizing the lessons of goodness and love in this world.

Brighter Days Ahead

With the youth of today, we hold our answers for tomorrow. Courtne, our former bus aide, loves Abigayle. She stays in touch with us, as Abigayle holds a deep place in her heart. She continually tells me Abigayle is her "other child." Her youngest daughter, Aliya, has grown up hearing about Abigayle and her struggles, as well as the work her mother does to care for children with developmental differences in her new role as an aide onsite.

At four years old, Aliya told her mother, "When I grow up, I want to work with Abigayle!" Courtne let me know that Aliya will be submitting her application in the next decade!!! To think that God is continually preparing new souls with desires to care for our most special of children and adults warms my heart. It gives me comfort that we will always find care for our Pink Snail Abigayle!

"And my God will meet all your needs according
to the riches of his glory in Christ Jesus."
Philippians 4:19 (NIV)

CHAPTER 13

MY PERSPECTIVE

"The difference between a mountain and
a molehill is your perspective."
Al Neuharth

WHEN LIFE'S SMOOTH, freshly paved road starts to feel more like a bumpy dirt road and shakes you up, open your eyes to find your life's purpose(s). My family's journey with Abigayle has been bumpy, and there is no reason for me to expect it to ever smooth out to the feeling of fresh pavement beneath us. I have grown fond of my bumpy road, as parenting Abigayle has provided unique challenges that have inspired me to work on solutions that can help families affected by autism and other sensory differences. When I see problems, I look for opportunities and solutions.

One thing I have learned through many years of experience parenting a child with autism is that no one truly "knows" autism. They only know the autism *they* have encountered. The struggle is real. It is gut-wrenching to hear the stories of what families endure, both the ones who care for their children in their home and those who have made the very hard decision to place their children in a residential program for their safety or other very personal reasons.

All I can share is that I do not judge any parent of a child with autism for their actions or choices. Even for those parents of children with less severe autism, it is a life that no one chooses or can prepare themselves to face fully. We all grow into it, as we cannot be fully equipped until we experience it and learn along the unique journey. It is hard to fit our children into a mold of expectations when they are unique, so I don't even pressure myself to try. This is true for children who do not have autism, too, but can be even harder with some of the characteristics within autism.

I've experienced love beyond expectations from both of my daughters, and for that, I am BLESSED. It has also been a tremendously fulfilling experience to watch my husband unselfishly give so much and sacrifice for his children. While Abigayle has severe autism and can display violent behaviors, she is also one of the most loving people in the world and gives the best physical expression of it (in between the tantrums). For this, I am thankful, as many other parents do not have the same experiences of affection, whether they have children with autism or not.

Life will go on, and autism will not break me. I imagine a life full of great gifts of love in my future. This is my focus: how my life will continue to advance. I will reach my goals through hard work and perseverance. My twins are my inspiration, and the lessons I have learned from being their mom will make me successful in fulfilling my dreams and life so much sweeter.

CHAPTER 14

WHEN IN DOUBT, JUST HAVE PATIENCE AND GIVE LOVE!

"Love is patient, love is kind. It does not envy, it does not boast, it is not proud. It does not dishonor others, it is not self-seeking, it is not easily angered, it keeps no record of wrongs."
1 Corinthians 13:4-5 (NIV)

WHEN IN DOUBT as to how you will make it through the day or how you will respond to the next difficult moment, remember that love will help all prevail above all else. When I mention love, I don't only mention love for others, but also love for thyself. In the most difficult of times, I turn to my faith and love.

"But I say to you, love your enemies and pray for those who persecute you."
Matthew 5:44 (ESV)

When we approach our circumstances, obstacles, and enemies with love, we will persevere with patience. We can manage the toughest of times through giving love. We are here on this earth to love and serve ourselves and others for a better life and future. Worry, struggle, and strife can be defeated with love. We can all be strengthened by love. The world can be made a better place by injecting more love into it.

"You also must be patient. Keep your hopes high, for the day of the Lord's coming is near."
James 5:8 (GNT)

There is freedom in patience. When I feel I am at my wits' end, I know that I am not alone … because I carry an endless supply of love, patience, support, and forgiveness with me everywhere I go. We alone cannot endure all that life throws our way, but our faith will ensure we prevail over the daily invaders of our happiness that try to strip away our courage, strength, and the goodness within.

We must rely on what is within. If we look within, we will always find the answers and the strength to go on another day and prevail. WE, collectively, have the strength and power to create a better world and existence for us all. WE, collectively, will prevail against the tough times and the daily invaders to our happiness as we give and receive more love!

> *"Beloved, never avenge yourselves, but leave it to the wrath of God, for it is written, 'Vengeance is mine, I will repay, says the Lord.'"*
> Romans 12:19 (ESV)

People try to create a level of importance through what they project to others, but don't be fooled—and don't fool yourself—as to your own relevance and impact on this world. You were meant to create impact on this exact moment in time, so don't doubt the relevance of what you can do and the impact you can have on the troubling times of today. Allow me to repeat that: you were specifically created to be relevant and impactful! Start today by being a life-lifter to others by sharing the love you have inside you. Try flashing a big smile every chance you get, and see how this improves your own mood.

> *What will you do with your gifts to create your own lines in our history books?*

CHAPTER 15

DOES IT ALL REALLY MATTER?

"For I know the plans I have for you," declares
the LORD, "plans to prosper you and not to harm
you, plans to give you hope and a future."
Jeremiah 29:11 (NIV)

I N THE END, what will we believe really mattered in our life? Is it the worry of the day or something else? Today, I may worry about never-ending bills, my former unappreciative boss, the disrespectful person I encountered, being tired, and that I don't have anything great to eat in the refrigerator for lunch. Today, I may go through the day replaying my problems instead of my gifts. Today, it may never occur to me to consider my neighbor with a dying spouse or my coworker who is alone and suffering from severe depression. I may live a spoiled, self-focused existence.

Abigayle's smile and Natalie's loving embrace are all it takes to bring me back into what matters most and remind me what's good in my life. In a split second, I return and rebalance myself. The love I experience from my girls opens my eyes to where I can share more love with others. I see Abigayle and Natalie as gifts that bring more to my life than any job or any perceived win in life.

We all have tremendous gifts right in front of us, waiting to be recognized for all that they are and can be for our lives. What are yours? What power do you have to create more for yourself? Be the exception by creating exceptional experiences for yourself and those you love. You can have and be more. What will you do today to ensure that happens?

Today, Make a Promise to Yourself

Today, make a promise to remember and remind yourself that you are more than your circumstances, weight, education, financial resources, experience, and current living conditions! You are more than your family's legacy! You are more than what you have shown in the past and more than what is visible to others! Today, you have infinite possibility to be more than you can imagine for yourself or others can imagine for you. You are part of a divine, limitless plan!

Today, make a promise to yourself to be more, love more, share more, give more, care more, forgive more, lift more (left up to your interpretation), experience more, feel more, absorb more, purge more unnecessary baggage, and be or do all other forms of MORE! Abigayle never accepts less than what she sees as hers to own, have, become, do, or otherwise. Her incredible tenacity and perseverance are an example for us all. Since I cannot reason with her in conversation, she just goes after what she wants and is quite successful in getting it. She decides for herself, on her timeline!

Today, consider what needs to be healed deeply within. Then, take the time and effort to let today be the last day that you are not healed or working on healing. For me, life can have long-term sustained periods of stress that throw me out of alignment. I have to fight to even recognize that I am and have been off-balance. Once I identify the problem, I fight to have a better experience of my life by healing the core of what is wrong. The silence in between life's busy moments is the most revealing for me. So, take some quiet time for yourself to gauge where you are and what you need in life to get where you need to go. We all must ask ourselves ... what is that destination?

Today, make a promise to yourself that it will be the last day you doubt what you can become. This will include not only holding the promise for yourself, but also creating boundaries for others who make you feel less. *You* hold the power to decide who you are and how you will carry yourself—and only *you*. Abigayle decides for herself every day. She shows the world what she will or will not do, despite the medical expertise or the limited mindset others sometimes have regarding her abilities. She shows the world, and you can too!

> *"Difficult roads often lead to beautiful*
> *destinations. The best is yet to come."*
> Zig Ziglar

CHAPTER 16

DON'T BE SCARED;
MAKE IT COUNT

God always shows up during times of impossibility in one way or another.

HONESTLY, I COULD easily justify living scared every day and every moment with Abigayle's severe autism. I could live scared of my hair being pulled as Abigayle drags me to the ground, a quick bite to my arm that will surely scar, a violent tantrum in public where I don't have control, or Abigayle getting away from me as she runs towards the street with cars. Life's dangers surround us (both those we see and those we don't), but Abigayle does not understand where the dangers are the way I do. I must be her "lifeguard" in life since she cannot do it for herself.

If I lived for what "could" happen every day and let it consume me, I would not have the great life that I do with Abigayle, nor would I be a great parent or wife. Also, I would not be able to hold down a successful job with great benefits that are critical to Abigayle's advancement. We are all given our roles in life; this one is mine and I am honored to fill it. I get so much more from Abigayle than what I give to her.

Early on, I had to learn to live without being scared that what is possible is probable. Through parenting Abigayle, I now see that what scares us can also be a blessing and part of our silver lining in life. The fight for Abigayle serves as a fight for humanity, as she helps teach us all to grow in our acceptance, tolerance, patience, flexibility, and true, unconditional love.

"God has a purpose for everything."
Inspired by Ezekiel 14:23[1]

---

[1] Jim Ellis and Lori Ellis, *Power Moments: Claim Your Identity – Book Within a Book* (McKinney, TX: Performance Publishing Group, 2020).

To me, the scariest reality would be to live scared instead of making my moments count! We all have many thousands of scary thoughts enter our mind, either through our own thinking or that of many loving and intelligent people around us. We cannot allow ourselves to live scared. Now, I am very careful and a rule follower, so there is a limit. That being said, I don't let the unknown keep me from exploring new opportunities or pathways to develop my experiences, knowledge, and passions.

Many caretakers have feared changing Abigayle's pull-on diapers. It could seem silly to think of this being an issue (I change her every single day, all day, without choice). This is when I remember to put myself in the shoes of others who are not her parents and recognize how it must be harder for them than it is for me. Abigayle thrives on taking power from those who show fear in caring for her. I can think of many sitters who were scared to approach Abigayle, and boy, did they miss out on some amazing loving. She is an incredible snuggler!

As we know, the things that scare us the most rarely end up happening. It is the things that we *never* consider that rock our world. Being scared and living in fear can have some value, but not when it is debilitating. Again, balance is key.

> *"Peace I leave with you; my peace I give to you.*
> *Not as the world gives do I give to you. Let not your*
> *hearts be troubled, neither let them be afraid."*
> John 14:27 (ESV)

CHAPTER 17

BEYOND THE BOUNDS

*If you just stay consistent, the little micro-efforts of
your everyday giving of love and other extra efforts can
create a life beyond the bounds of your imagination!*

S OMETIMES I WONDER why adults did not tell me how it would
be growing up, but then I consider myself thankful that I was
oblivious to what was in store. I often remind myself that the good
times would not all exist or taste so sweet without the struggle of the
hard times. If I knew of the hard times on my path, I surely would have
tried to avoid a few people and circumstances here and there that got
me to where I need to be at this very moment ... writing this book.

Looking back from today, can I tell myself that it was all worth
the struggle? I can, but it still feels bad as I go through the more
challenging times of loss, struggle, fear, exhaustion, and more. This
is where I resort back to my faith and the bigger picture beyond my
current awareness of the value in our existence. I know there is so
much more to life than what I can see and feel today.

*We are all pioneers raging through uncharted
waters, as each life is uniquely special, and
we are forging into the unknown.*

The bigger picture in life—beyond the bounds of what I can see
and know—helps me understand there is a reason for everything and
that everything will turn out for the good of all. Focusing beyond the
bounds of my imagination gives me strength in times of weakness.
The bigger picture tells me to be patient, because there is more to
come, and it is not all bad. The bigger picture is where I need to
focus, while also treasuring every moment in between. Sometimes,

prevailing over the hard days is as simple as just reminding myself that I am not alone in the struggle.

"The troubles that surround me belong to God!"
Inspired by Numbers 31:2[2]

As you know, childhood is fleeting, so I better get all I can from the lessons Natalie and Abigayle are teaching me as they grow into this world. They are the best teachers. Who knew that we don't just teach our kids, but we are also taught by them?

Abigayle and Natalie educate me daily as a parent, but also as a person. They stretch me to be a better person. I look for these moments in life when times are tough and ask myself, "Am I proud of my response as their role model?" I ask myself, "Am I carrying myself in a way that I feel confident is the most loving and generous way?" I know when I am being petty or unfair to others. It does not happen often, but there are times when the bad actions of others bring out the worst in me. When I find myself off track, I try to gain a different perspective and regroup. After all, I am the example for my children.

"Don't worry that children never listen to you;
worry that they are always watching you."
Robert Fulghum

---

[2]   Jim Ellis and Lori Ellis, *Power Moments.*

BLOSSOMING

our beautiful girl

When things feel outside of what we can absorb or manage within ourselves, the answer is always the same. Look beyond your bounds, and turn to God. We should consider God's perspective when our own is not positive or comforting to us. Especially in the most difficult of times, we should change the way we look at the problem or situation. We should ask ourselves how Jesus would see the same and respond.

"But he who is joined to the Lord
becomes one spirit with him."
1 Corinthians 6:17 (ESV)

"For by grace you have been saved through faith.
And this is not your own doing; it is the gift of God,
not a result of works, so that no one may boast."
Ephesians 2:8-9 (ESV)

Thank You!

Thank you for taking the time to read this material. I've loved sharing my life as the parent of a child diagnosed with autism—both the joys and struggles—and the lessons learned. I hope the time you've spent reading the life lessons creates value for you in your life too. Life is hard, but we all must keep growing and moving forward.

"Turn your wounds into wisdom."
Oprah Winfrey

There have been many years of my life where I have disappointed myself and allowed myself to waste time in a rut or hold on to toxicity from my life choices or feelings of unworthiness. I, like you, have struggled with bad habits—which in my case caused the extra pounds to pile on my body. I now know that I did this because something was wrong inside of me and not because I loved food or drinking caloric drinks. Because I did not value myself as the miracle I now know I am, I wasted many years, moments, and opportunities.

I did not think that I deserved more, so maybe it was a form of punishment not to treat myself with white-glove service, as if I deserved less. I now know that I am invaluable, despite those who like to judge me as otherwise. You too deserve every magical thing that the world can offer, as well as incredible health and vibrancy. So, no matter where you are right now on your journey, take time with these lessons and the questions at the end of each lesson to see what it is that may be holding you back from a more incredible life. There is always more for you. It's time to collect on it!

Remember, life is full of richness all around us when we just look for it—so start looking!

"I can do all this through Him who gives me strength."
Philippians 4:13 (NIV)

God bless us all!

Please continue to read the remaining pages of this book, as I share incredible stories of many unsung heroes trying to make this world a better place. They too have encountered trying circumstances in life and have risen to the challenge to be more, do more, love more, create more, give more, and beyond!

If you found this book valuable, consider visiting my website (https://kimberlykelsoe.com) for more of my writing on multiple topic areas. On the website, you can find free downloadable materials to advance your life. I also look forward to hearing from you via social media forums or through my website and email.

APPENDIX I

Lessons Learned: Through No Words At All

My Favorite Life Lesson: Don't be so hard on yourself

Premier Life Lesson: Having the right perspective is as good as gold

- The little things matter
- Life is grand, if you don't know any better
- You don't always get what you "think" you want or need, but it is important to embrace what you have
- Life is imperfect and out of your control, so you might as well keep moving forward

"HERE and NOW" Matters Most

- Focus on high priority and greatest impact
- It is not what we go through in a day that can drain us, but what our *mind* goes through in a day ...
- Planning is pertinent
- It is critical to develop and maintain faith and trust within yourself

External Influences Are on the Outside ... Keep Them There

- There is a lot of noise around. Block it out!
- Dismiss the judgment of others as ignorance
- Bad vibes emanate from bad people
- Saving myself is all up to me ... and God, of course!
- Self-preservation and boundaries are a must

Everyone Impacts Their Surroundings

- The ability to share and learn is a gift no one should take for granted

APPENDIX II

Unsung Heroes of Autism and More

I have met so many incredible people who are transforming the world and supporting our children with learning differences. It is even more inspiring to see parents encountering a diagnosis and not giving up or giving in to it. They have chosen to serve and support others in similar situations instead. The diagnosis of autism has been a spark for many. They change their lives completely to create solutions for their children and their community by starting schools, foundations, and more.

You too can be a hero for your troubles. If something is troubling you, ask yourself what you can do to help solve the problem for others encountering the same. Is this "trouble" tied to your purpose in life? There is a reason you are experiencing this challenge or difficulty. What is the experience trying to tell you? The inspiring stories below are an inspiration for me to keep looking into my problems, rather than turning away from them in hopes they will disappear.

South Walton Academy

Calley Middlebrooks, mother of three, has been an amazing example for mothers with children on the spectrum and neuro-typical children. She and her close friend, Jennifer Filippone, saw unmet needs in their community for individualized curriculums to get the most out of the time spent and for our children's future. They took action when they saw a need, despite their own personal demands and challenges.

Calley, an Intervention Specialist, had a son diagnosed with autism at four years of age. After having worked with children and families for years to navigate the system of services, she decided to start a school to support the community. The school is a tremendous success and continues to grow in leaps and bounds. They really put their heart into their work, and it shows. I have never seen Abigayle advance more and be happier than at South Walton Academy.

Calley and Jennifer have been true angels on this earth for Abigayle. Without their willingness to push the limits and have open dialogue regarding solutions, Abigayle would likely not have a place to attend therapy and school. This would have been devastating to our family and have long-term impacts on society, as Abigayle is growing in her functioning every day through the comprehensive services they are individualizing at South Walton Academy for her care. I thought of doing the same when I ran up against roadblocks in care for Abigayle, but God led us to this wonderful place, and I will forever be grateful.

Calley and Jennifer followed their calling in life and prospered. They are true inspirations for putting ourselves out there and taking a chance to serve and create a better world for others. They have succeeded. South Walton Academy has been such a treasure find for our family. I am excited to see it continue to grow in ways that support Abigayle and many other children like her. If you are looking for an impactful non-profit organization to contribute to, consider South Walton Academy.

If you want to learn more about the wonderful work they are doing and contribute to their cause, please visit them at https://www.southwaltonacademy.com. Your time and resources will pay off if you contribute to a scholarship or enhanced facilities and more.

Letter from Calley, President of South Walton Academy ...

The moment I met Abigayle I knew we had to have her. Our program was not quite set up for the accommodations she needed, but that is the whole purpose of our program: to meet needs not being met. The first day of working with Abigayle, she tested our team to see which of us were worth working for. By the end of her first session, we were all exhausted. We put minimal requests on her, and as she intentionally did the work incorrectly, she looked up and grinned. It took some work and a few lost strands of hair, but by the end of her first session, she completed an activity and felt proud. Ah, success! As we walked her out to leave, Abigayle gave me a kiss. She may not have liked the work, but she understood and could feel that we were here to help her.

As a mom of a child with autism, I know the challenges our children face, their siblings face, and we as parents face—the looks people give, the parties that siblings miss out on—but at the end of the day the only thing I would change would be making life easier on our children. Being able to give them the tools to be successful, in whatever capacity they are able. I'm happy we can be a part of your journey and grateful that you share Abigayle with us. We have an amazing team of therapists and teachers who all want success for our Abigayle and all of our students. They are constantly looking for ways to better each unique need.

Kimberly, thank you for sharing your story. Your positivity and lessons learned are very well put.

Calley Middlebrooks
Founder | President | Developmental Therapist
South Walton Academy, Inc.
Non-Profit | Private Elementary School & Therapy Center
Santa Rosa Beach, Florida
www.southwaltonacademy.com

Growing Together Behavioral Center

Melissa Kramer and her husband Matt are parents to four amazing children adopted from China and South Korea. After learning of the great therapies out there for her youngest son, Aiden, Melissa recognized the need for more quality resources in her local community. I know people who have moved to be nearer to resources, but Melissa chose to solve the issue of lack of resources instead of moving.

I hope one day that Melissa tells her entire story and journey with her children, but until then, I can tell you that she is a leader of leaders in resilience, compassion, and love. Melissa has endured one crisis after another, each of which on its own would bring a stronger person than I am to their knees. She endures it all, while taking the time to inspire and serve others for a better way and better lives.

Melissa and Matt both have spirits to serve, even though their circumstances within their family give them more than enough to do. They still serve their communities in numerous ways besides starting the Growing Together Behavioral Center. They are proof that life breaks you down or builds you up. They are builders, and we can all watch them as a positive example of how the diagnosis of autism can create greatness in lives.

You should definitely check out the incredible work they are doing in their community and how they are expanding the scope of what they can accomplish in serving others through their vision for more. To learn more about the Growing Together Behavioral Center or how you can help them make a broader impact, please visit https://gtbjax.org.

Westonwood Ranch

Lindy Wood shared with me her incredible story of sacrifice and perseverance after discovering that her son Weston has autism. The story touched me, but her mission is even more touching. Lindy is an example of a mom who will do anything for her children, including sacrificing a normal family life for a chance at a better life for one of her children.

After greatly sacrificing time with her family during the early days, and with a newborn in tow, Lindy and her family moved to another state to get the best therapies for her son. The therapies were working, but Weston was capable of so much more. Lindy recognized an opportunity to advance Weston's therapies to include a more holistic learning program that would help him develop job skills in a natural setting.

She started Westonwood Ranch to create an opportunity for others, like Weston, to advance in new ways and support their exposure to skills that can create a career path. I had the privilege to visit the ranch right before they opened the school. I saw the sensory room, exercise room, art studio (to create art to sell), kitchen, and horses. Her vision was incredibly well thought-out, and the blessings were there to follow. I was amazed by what she'd created.

Lindy has created something so unique and incredible, but her vision is for more. There are still so many more unmet needs for children who grow out of the programs and who need additional residential options due to aging parents and/or advancing aggression. I look forward to watching all that this facility will accomplish. If you are interested in learning more or finding opportunities to volunteer or contribute to the incredible work Westonwood Ranch is doing, please visit https://www.westonwood.org.

Caretaking Is for the Strong

There are many, many unsung heroes serving as caretakers for others within this community. Caretakers are special angels put on this earth to serve with the incredible skills of strength, love, and patience. I would be remiss if I did not recognize the heroic efforts of those who give their time and energy voluntarily. Abigayle has many angels who have shown up at just the right time to offer a helping hand, some of whom I have mentioned in this book. These caretakers have been there for Abigayle and the rest of my family. There are days when they have shown up to care for Abigayle, but they also took the time to counsel me. I have often told people that caretakers for Abigayle do it for the love of our family and Abigayle, as they certainly can find easier ways to make money!

We can all learn and grow from being around each other. One of my greatest lessons in how I manage the struggles that come with caring for Abigayle during a tantrum came from Courtne, her school aide. Courtne taught me to separate Abigayle from the diagnosis of autism. You can address the autism, but the autism is not the child.

This helped me have a new perspective and made me understand that it can be easy to let go after the tantrums. It has also helped me in other situations throughout life. The lesson of separating certain behaviors from a person has been a tremendous gift.

How can you follow the example of our unsung heroes of autism and create change in this world?

If you are wondering what you can do to make a difference in life, ask yourself if there is an unmet need in the world that you see. I ask myself, "What do I want and need to read?" and then I start writing. Are you following your passions and creating more in this world? If not, the time to start is today.

Start expecting miracles with a determined knowing that they are on their way to you. Look all around for them. They will appear in hidden corners or glare brightly just ahead on your path... right on time! All you have to do is look. Then, give thanks and get back to looking for more!